THE ETERNAL LITURGY

A Study Guide to the Video Film
The Divine Liturgy of St. John Chrysostom

Produced by

The Greek Orthodox Archdiocese
Department of Religious Education

Theodore Stylianopoulos

To my daughter Kiriaki Claire

That she and all young people may love the Liturgy and present themselves as "a living sacrifice" to the Lord (Rom. 12:1)

Illustrations by John G. Hamwey

ISBN 0-86687-068-7

CONTENTS

PREFACE   vii

A WORD TO THE READER   ix

1. PREPARING TO VIEW THE VIDEO   1

2. THE LITURGY OF THE WORD   5
   The Meaning of the Liturgy   6
   Preparations for the Liturgy   8
   Active Participation in the Liturgy   11
   The Content of the Liturgy of the Word   14
   Application of the Liturgy   21

3. THE EUCHARIST   23
   The Great Entrance   25
   The Offering of the Gifts (Anaphora)   29
   The Lord's Prayer   36
   Holy Communion   46
   The Dismissal   51

4. RENEWAL THROUGH THE LITURGY   56
   What Is Renewal?   56
   Attitudes to the Liturgy   60
   Spiritual Re-awakening   63
   Three Urgent Goals   65

5. THEOLOGICAL AND HISTORICAL REFLECTIONS
   ON THE LITURGY   72
   The Essence of the Liturgy   72
   The Names of the Liturgy   76
   The Historical Growth and Structure of the Liturgy   84

6. HOW TO USE THIS STUDY GUIDE   91
   Two Session Program   91
   One Day Retreat   93
   Multiple Session Program   93
   Discussion Questions   94

BIBLIOGRAPHY   104

Other works of Father Theodore Stylianopoulos available through the Religious Education Department include:

COME RECEIVE THE LIGHT BIBLE STUDIES I–II

YEAR OF THE LORD: LITURGICAL BIBLE STUDIES 1–5

BREAD FOR LIFE: READING THE BIBLE

CHRIST IN OUR MIDST: SPIRITUAL RENEWAL IN THE ORTHODOX CHURCH

MY ORTHODOX PRAYERBOOK

PREFACE

Personal prayer is the most sublime experience of the believing soul. Corporate worship is the most profound activity of the Church as a faith community. In both personal prayer and corporate worship the risen Christ comes to us. We participate in the saving acts of His life. He touches our minds and hearts so that our life may be continuously renewed in His likeness. We become alive to His presence. We rejoice in the loving fellowship which He freely offers to us. "Behold, I stand at the door and knock; if any one hears my voice and opens the doors, I will come in to him and eat with him, and he with me" (Rev. 3:20).

The Divine Liturgy is the focus of prayer and worship. The Liturgy is the sacred rite by which the Orthodox Church celebrates the mystery of the Eucharist, derived from the words and actions of the Lord Jesus Christ at the Last Supper. It is the central mystery of the Church, the source and summit of its life. Through the Liturgy the Church is continuously changed from a human community into the body of Christ, the temple of the Holy Spirit, the holy people of God. Every sacrament transforms us into members of the body of Christ, but the Eucharist effects this most perfectly through Holy Communion. Christ's life is infused into ours. The risen Christ comes to dwell in us, casting out sin and corruption and bringing to us healing and immortal life. Because of the Liturgy we can all say, in some measure, with St. Paul: "It is no longer I who live, but Christ who lives in me" (Gal. 2:20).

I am delighted by the publication of *The Eternal Liturgy*, a beautifully written book that presents the richness of the Divine Liturgy as it relates to the everyday life of Orthodox Christians. Father Theodore Sylianopoulos, scholar, teacher and priest, has prepared a thorough and helpful guide for the study of the Liturgy. This book is readable, simple, and deep in content. Any interested reader will benefit from its valuable insights and practical guidance. Reading it is a special treat for all those who seek to be touched by the inexhaustible mystery of Christ, lived and celebrated through the Divine Liturgy.

Father Alkiviadis C. Calivas,
Dean and Professor of Liturgics
Hellenic College/Holy Cross Greek Orthodox
School of Theology

A WORD TO THE READER

When Jesus, tired and thirsty from His journey, sat by the well of Jacob to rest, the Samaritan woman refused to give Him a drink. But Jesus offered her "living water," a gift of God which becomes in those who drink of it "a spring of water welling up to eternal life" (Jn 4:10,15). The Christ who is the same yesterday and today continues to offer us this living water through the Liturgy. The Divine Liturgy is a spiritual Jacob's well at which wearied travelers can be refreshed and regain strength for life's journey by receiving anew the gift of the Holy Spirit. "If any one thirst, let him come to me and drink. He who believes in me, as the Scripture has said, 'Out of his heart shall flow rivers of living water.' Now this He said about the Spirit..." (Jn 7:37-38).

Life is a journey of joys and burdens; and sometimes, so it seems, more burdens than joys. We need regular times of refreshment and renewal of strength and vision. Nothing can compare with the richness of the Divine Liturgy, this magnificent treasure of Orthodox worship, the most frequent spiritual event in which all Orthodox Christians can participate. As the Divine Liturgy is the center of Orthodox life, so also it is the primary opportunity for Orthodox spiritual renewal. Every baptized Orthodox Christian is invited by Christ to partake regularly of the crystal waters of the Spirit which He Himself as the Chief Celebrant gives through the Liturgy. Whoever truly thirsts and desires can bring her or his cup and take as much water as it can hold. A small cup will hold little water, a large one will hold much. The benefit a person draws from the Divine Liturgy will be according to his or her faith and spiritual striving both in and outside of the Liturgy. The world today offers a lot of swampwater infested with faithless, materialistic, and purely humanistic values, where many wretched people try vainly to quench their thirst. But Christ invites all of us, dear reader, to partake of the living water of His grace and love. Listen to His voice. Come, drink from the abundant waters of the spiritual fountain of the eternal Liturgy.[1]

This small book is a modest contribution to the ongoing challenge of Orthodox spiritual renewal in our own times and circumstances. Its main purpose is that of a Study Guide accompanying the instructional video film "The Divine Liturgy of St. John Chrysostom" produced by the Religious Education Department of the Greek Orthodox Archdiocese of North and South America. It is primarily intended for priests, retreat leaders, Church school teachers, and discussion facilitators to help them in presenting and discussing the video film with various groups

---

[1]Some of the images and ideas of this paragraph come from Augustines Kantiotes, *On The Divine Liturgy*, Vol. 1, transl. by A. Gerostergios (1986), pp. 264-265.

and in different settings. Chapters 1-3 can selectively be used as the actual text in introducing and presenting the film in a flexible program ranging from two to as many as twelve sessions depending on need and opportunity. Chapters 4 and 5 provide further enrichment: Chapter 4 deals with the issue of personal renewal through the Liturgy as a central thrust in Orthodox spiritual renewal, while Chapter 5 gives additional background on the theology and structure of the Divine Liturgy. Chapter 6 offers detailed instructions about how to use this Study Guide in connection with the video film.

Although this book is primarily intended to accompany the video film, it can be used in other ways. All Orthodox have participated in the Divine Liturgy and are at least generally familiar with it. Any Orthodox or even other interested reader casually familiar with the Orthodox Liturgy can, therefore, gain new insights by reading this book. Too, he or she might be inspired to go to the Liturgy more frequently and to participate more meaningfully. Of course one can obtain the video itself and view it at home with family members or friends. Moreover, the illustrations and insights of this book can be useful to priests, educators, youth workers, and parents in other ways, such as in sermons, talks, class discussions, and personal conversations in our urgent contemporary need to heighten our consciousness both to the value and practice of the Liturgy.

Many thanks to Father Alkiviadis Calivas, Dean and Professor of Liturgics of Hellenic College and Holy Cross Greek Orthodox School of Theology from whom I have over the years learned much about the Liturgy, and who would himself have written this book had it not been for his myriad duties especially during the Holy Cross 50th Anniversary celebrations of 1986-1987. I am grateful to him for taking the time to review the manuscript and to write the preface. Ernest Villas, Director of the Religious Education Department, has greatly encouraged me with his counsel and criticism during our weekly discussions to complete this project. I also express gratitude to my Presvytera Fotini for her usual careful editorial work. The translation of the Liturgy used in the video film and in this book is that by faculty members of Holy Cross Greek Orthodox School of Theology.

Theodore Stylianopoulos

Professor of New Testament
Holy Cross Greek Orthodox School of Theology
and Theological Consultant to the Religious
Education Department, Greek Orthodox
Archdiocese of North and South America

Feast of THE THREE HIERARCHS
January 30, 1988

1

PREPARING TO VIEW THE VIDEO

This video program on the Divine Liturgy of St. John Chrysostom you are about to see was produced by the Religious Education Department of the Greek Orthodox Archdiocese and was filmed on the campus of Hellenic College and Holy Cross Greek Orthodox School of Theology. It features faculty members and students of the Seminary. The congregation represents members of the Seminary community and local Orthodox Christians who came to worship on the day the Liturgy was filmed. The video consists of two half-hour parts and presents highlights of the Liturgy, interviews with faculty and students, and classroom instruction.

Before viewing the video, it may be helpful to sit back and collect our thoughts by reflecting briefly on the importance of the Liturgy for our lives. We begin with a true story about the early Christians.

Around 112 AD a persecution had broken out against Christians in Bithynia, a province on the north western coast of Asia Minor. Accused Christians— men, women, and even youths— were interrogated by Pliny, the Roman governor, who officially charged them to renounce their faith, curse Christ, and worship the emperor's statue or be executed. What crime had they committed? What was their guilt? In Pliny's own words from his letter to the emperor:

> The whole of their guilt...was that they were in the habit of meeting on a certain fixed day before it was light, when they sang in alternate verses a hymn to Christ, as to a god, and bound themselves by a solemn oath, not to do any wicked deeds...never to commit any fraud, theft or adultery, never to falsify their word...[1]

Although their high morals were unquestioned, Christians were persecuted and killed for gathering to celebrate the Divine Liturgy!

What is the Liturgy? Why have faithful Orthodox Christians at different times in ancient and modern

---

[1] Pliny's entire letter to Emperor Trajan and Trajan's reply may be found in *A New Eusebius*, ed. J. Stevenson (London: SPCK, 1965), pp. 13–16.

history risked even their lives to worship Christ through the Liturgy? What does the Liturgy mean to you personally?

As you know, the Divine Liturgy goes back to the Last Supper. It is the most precious gift which we have received from the hands of Jesus Himself. When Christ approached the time of His passion, He had a special meal with His closest followers. Through solemn words and actions He showed to them the meaning of His life and death. He took bread and gave it to them, saying: "Take, eat; this is my body." Again He gave to them a cup, saying: "Drink of it, all of you; for this is my blood of the new covenant, which is poured out for many for the forgiveness of sins" (Mt. 26:26-29). Then He also commanded them to continue this sacred meal: "Do this in remembrance of me" (Lk. 22:19; 1 Cor. 11:24).

Through these words and actions Jesus signified not only the meaning of His redemptive sacrifice on the Cross but also an intimate mystical communion that He would continue to have with His followers through this special meal. Indeed, the deepest mystery of the Liturgy is the risen Christ Himself sharing Himself personally with us through the gifts of bread and wine. As He said to His disciples and to others at an another time: "He who eats my flesh and drinks my blood has eternal life...[he] abides in me, and I in him" (Jn 7:54,56).

The value of the Liturgy is summed up by Bishop Augoustinos Kantiotes of Florina, Greece. In a work recently translated into English and highly recommended for further meditation on the Liturgy, Bishop Augoustinos writes:

> The Divine Liturgy is a mystery: it is the mystery of mysteries. If the Lord enlightens our minds and enflames our hearts, so that we can hear and participate in this mystery, then we cannot remain cold and indifferent to it. Instead, a deeply felt gratitude towards our great benefactor, the Triune God (Father, Son, and Holy Spirit), will reign in our hearts.[2]

Do we as Orthodox Christians truly recognize the treasure we have in the Divine Liturgy? There is a story about a jewel and a jewel box. Once a noble family came into possession of a priceless jewel and in order to safeguard it, put it in a beautiful jewelbox. The next generation valued not only the jewel but also the jewelbox, and so they placed both in another beautiful jewelbox of larger size. After many generations and many jewelboxes, the outside jewelbox itself, made of delicate carvings and decorated with costly gems, was universally acknowledged as a masterpiece. One day an admiring visitor asked: "What's in the jewelbox?" The question took people by surprise. A few knew the answer. But many were quite uncertain. Still others did not even know at all what the magnificent jewelbox contained!

Cannot this story of the jewel and the jewelbox be applied to the Divine Liturgy as it has been handed down by generations of Orthodox Christians? The Liturgy is both the jewel and the jewelbox. As the jewel it is the same gift of Christ originally given to the Apostles and received in the Eucharist. As the jewelbox the Liturgy consists of the developed prayers, dramatic actions, and music— an exquisite creation of beauty and dignity seeking to express the inestimable value of the jewel.

---

[2] *On the Divine Liturgy*, Vol. 1, p. 14.

But do we fully appreciate the value of the content as well as the beauty of the Liturgy? What is your understanding of the Liturgy? What do you say when a visitor asks you, "what does the word 'Liturgy' mean?" or, "what is the Liturgy all about?" or, "why is the Liturgy so important for the Orthodox?" Do you know the main parts of the Liturgy? Can you explain, if asked, what a particular act in the Liturgy means, for example, the procession of the Holy Gospel Book which is plated with gold or silver? Why is it plated with gold or silver? Why is the Liturgy also called Eucharist? What is the meaning of the *antidoron* (blessed bread) given to all at the end of the Liturgy?

Many of these questions pertain to the knowledge you may have acquired about the Liturgy. But now what of your true feelings regarding the Liturgy? Do you get anything out of it? What do you get? Do you come on time or late for the Liturgy? Why or why not? Are you refreshed and strengthened, or bored and tired by the Liturgy? What do you feel is your role in the Liturgy? Does the Liturgy make any real difference in your daily life? How do you relate the Liturgy to your personal life? How do you prepare for the Liturgy? Do you receive Holy Communion frequently, periodically, or rarely? Why or why not? What is your relationship to other Christians in the Liturgy? Is the Liturgy for you an experience of Christ or a routine religious rite? Would you, if necessary, risk significant hardship or even danger to your life in order to be present at the Liturgy?

Keeping these questions in mind, let's view the first half hour of the video. After viewing it, we can discuss these and similar questions. Our prayer is that, by God's grace, our knowledge and experience of the Liturgy will be enriched as a result of these sessions.

2

THE LITURGY OF THE WORD

We have seen the first half of the video presentation on the Liturgy. It concentrated on the first part of the Liturgy which is called, as the film pointed out, the Liturgy of the Word. Probably most of us felt like visitors to the campus of Hellenic College/Holy Cross. We experienced something of the celebration of the Liturgy by the priests and students of our Seminary. We heard their comments about the meaning of the Liturgy, as well as their feelings toward the Liturgy. The Byzantine music, the seminary chapel's iconography and architecture, the seminary surroundings, all filled our minds and hearts with many impressions.

What are your own impressions about what you saw and heard? If you were to choose one or two main points to talk about, what would they be? Did you learn some new things about the Liturgy? What are they? What did you think of the seminarians speaking about their difficulties in concentrating and actively participating during the Liturgy? How can these difficulties be dealt with? Now that you have seen the first half of the video program, how would you define the Liturgy? What would you say the Liturgy is all about? In what ways do you connect the Liturgy with your life?

(Note to study leaders: If you have scheduled only one group session of sixty minutes or less for the first half of the video program, discussion of the above questions and other similar questions on p. 4 should immediately follow the viewing of the video. If more sessions and/or more time have been scheduled, see the instructions in chapter 6).

The first part of the video program touched on a number of important points: (1) The Meaning of the Liturgy; (2) Preparations for the Liturgy; (3) Active Participation in the Liturgy; (4) The Content of the Liturgy of the Word; and (5) Applications of the Liturgy. Let's meditate on and discuss each of these points.

The Meaning of the Liturgy

The narrator of the video likened the Liturgy to "a jewel among the treasures of Orthodox worship." The word "jewel" conveys both extraordinary beauty and priceless value. Why is the Liturgy so important? Let's consider first the fundamental meaning of the Liturgy— what we may call the building blocks of a "theology" of the Liturgy.

St. Luke the Evangelist tells the story of the two disciples, whom tradition later identified as Luke and Cleopas, walking from Jerusalem to Emmaus after the resurrection of Jesus (Lk. 24:13-35). The risen Lord joined them. He listened to them compassionately. He set their hearts on fire with His words. He made Himself known to them through the breaking of bread in a mystical way. "He took bread and blessed, and broke it, and gave it to them. And their eyes were opened and they recognized Him" (Lk. 24:30-31). Then He vanished from their midst.

What happened on that walk from Jerusalem to Emmaus is an image of our own journey in the Liturgy. As we celebrate the Liturgy, the living Christ comes in our midst. We acknowledge Him as our God and Savior. We pray to Him. He listens to our prayers and cleanses us with His grace. He gives Himself to us as the bread of life and reveals Himself to us in the Eucharist. He sets our hearts on fire with the divine love of the Father and the renewing power of the Holy Spirit. Though He again vanishes from our midst, our eyes are opened. We have a new vision of ourselves, each other, our fellow human beings, and all creation.

The priceless jewel of the Liturgy is Christ Himself. The heart of the Liturgy is our personal meeting with the risen Christ, a gift more valuable than all the wealth of the earth. All the theological meaning of the Liturgy is to be found in this, that the Liturgy is a remembrance and celebration of the saving ministry of Christ— His birth, life, death, resurrection, ascension and second coming. What we proclaim as the good news of the

Gospel, we celebrate sacramentally through the Liturgy. Not only do we celebrate it but we also share in it. We re-live the saving events of the life of Christ and we look to His return in His glorious kingdom.

Christ Himself is the mystical Celebrant of the Liturgy. He invites us to be participants in the Last Supper. We praise and glorify him, together with the Father and the Holy Spirit. We dare approach the table of His love. We are united with Him and with each other as His mystical body. We commit our lives to Him. As the risen Lord, He sends us forth to continue His mission and to be His witnesses in the world by the power of the Holy Spirit.

Do you recall some of the specific references to Christ made by people appearing in the video? Commenting on the vesting of the priest, Father Ilia Katre said that the priest, as he is vesting and reciting appropriate prayers, "is transformed into the image of Christ, who is the Celebrant, the High Priest" of the Liturgy. Deacon Constantine Pappademos explained that the hymns of the Liturgy are "evangelical and doctrinal; evangelical in that they proclaim the Gospel...and doctrinal in that they proclaim the basic beliefs of our Faith" about God, salvation, and life. Father Theodore Stylianopoulos noted that the procession and lifting up of the Gospel Book during the Small Entrance symbolize "the importance of the teachings of Christ and His Word;" and that, a little later in the Liturgy, when the Gospel is read, "the congregation hears the words of the Gospel as if they were being uttered by Christ Himself," and we praise Him: "Glory to You, O Lord, glory to You!"

It is clear that the Divine Liturgy is far more than a beautiful ceremony or even a religious obligation which we as Orthodox Christians must fulfill. It is a sharing in the mystery of the living Christ here and now— *our own Emmaus experience* as often as we meet to conduct the Liturgy today. The Liturgy celebrates our new life in Christ. The Liturgy reflects the centrality of Christ in the Church. Just as Christ is the living Head and Source of His followers who make up His body, so also the Liturgy is, as the video narrator put it, "the very center of the life of the Church." Therefore, to use again the words of the narrator, "the Liturgy is the spiritual fountain of the Church, the feast of new creation in

Jesus Christ." Through the Liturgy we receive the blessings and benefits of Christ's saving work.

Through the Liturgy we experience most intimately the renewing power of the mystical presence of God's kingdom. Through the Liturgy we also express our gratitude to God for His glorious saving deeds and His redeeming grace. The Liturgy is our way of thanking God, praising Him and glorifying Him. As our prayerful, doxological response to God for all His blessings, the Liturgy is a fervent prayer of thanksgiving for His Son, our forgiveness, new life, and the gift of the Spirit richly bestowed upon us by our loving Father. The Liturgy is truly a "Eucharist" (Thanksgiving).

(Note to study leaders: Chapter 5 elaborates further on the theological meaning of the Liturgy).

Preparations for the Liturgy

An interesting scene in the video was the ringing of the Seminary chapel bell. The ringing of a Church bell has symbolic significance. Of course bells sound for many reasons—jubilation, mourning, or danger. But when a bell rings for worship it is a clear call to gather for the most significant activity of life— the praise and glorification of God for His majesty, goodness, and love toward creation. Everyone can hear the bell's sound. Everyone is called. A ringing Church bell symbolizes God's universal call to salvation for God "desires all to be saved and to come to the knowledge of the truth" (1 Tim. 2:4).

The Divine Liturgy is a call. Through the Liturgy God calls us to pray to Him and to grow in our communion with Him. When the Seminary chapel bell was ringing in the video the narrator commented: "At every Liturgy, we hear God's call and gather to worship Him in the spirit of joy and thanksgiving." Do we truly gather "in the spirit of joy and thanksgiving?" Are we ready and eager to put our hearts into the worship of God? Can we hear God's call through the Liturgy as clearly as we can hear the Church bell? Speaking honestly we must admit that often this is not the case. Just as we may not pay much attention to the sound waves of a Church bell, so also our preoccupied consciousness may not be much stirred by the spiritual vibrations of the Liturgy.

What, then, can be done? The answer to this question is found in two key words: preparation and participation. Let's see first what preparation means for hearing God's call through the Liturgy. There are several kinds of preparation to keep in mind.

One kind of preparation is the liturgical rhythm, the cycle of prayers and services of the total life of the Church. The Liturgy is not meant to be celebrated in isolation. Although it is a distinct unit in itself, it is also related to the seasons and feasts of the liturgical year, as well as to other worship services in the daily liturgical cycle. For example, the video pointed out that the Orthodox liturgical day begins at sunset with Vespers, a service of psalms, prayers, and particular hymns related to the feast being celebrated. In addition, prior to the Liturgy, the morning service of Matins, an even richer service of psalms, prayers, and hymns, is offered. We should not forget, as well, the cycle of private evening, morning and other prayers, most importantly, the prayers in preparation for Holy Communion, appointed for Orthodox Christians in Orthodox prayerbooks. All these feasts, services, and prayers have been established by the Church to embrace our whole life with the spirit of worship and prayer. The whole liturgical rhythm of the Church, when we stay in touch with it, helps us to be prepared and stay prepared for the celebration of the Liturgy.

Another kind of preparation is specific for the Liturgy and involves primarily the priest. In the liturgical books the full title of the Liturgy is "The Order of the Divine and Holy Liturgy." The word "Order" here implies several brief services conducted prior to what the Orthodox faithful usually recognize as the beginning of the Liturgy with the invocation "Blessed is the Kingdom..." The video mentioned "many preparatory acts and services" prior to the celebration of the Liturgy. Among them are: (a) The Service of the *Kairos* (Appointed Time), consisting of preparatory prayers of the priest; (b) The Service of Vesting, prayers offered by the priest as he puts on his sacred vestments; and (c) The Service of the *Proskomide* (Preparation of the Gifts), during which the gifts of bread and wine are prepared to be taken to the Altar Table for consecration later on in the Liturgy.

All these services are actually part of the whole cycle of the Liturgy but only the *preparatory parts* which are conducted privately by the priest. Nevertheless they contain profound meaning and deserve close examination (in a more detailed study of the Liturgy which cannot be pursued here). These preparatory parts have not only practical intent, that is, for the priest to arrive early, be properly vested, and have the gifts of bread and wine prepared for consecration; they have also personal meaning for the priest, helping him to prepare in heart and mind for the celebration of the Liturgy. For example, as Father Ilia Katre mentioned in the video, vesting reflects the beauty of new creation and reminds the priest that he is transformed in the image of Christ, the true Celebrant of the Liturgy. This is a most inspiring, perhaps overwhelming, thought for the priest as he prepares for the Liturgy!

Are there preparatory acts also intended for lay persons as they come to the Liturgy? Yes, it is important for each Orthodox Christian to prepare himself or herself to hear God's call through the Liturgy in several ways. Acts of Orthodox piety, such as lighting a candle and venerating an icon when entering the Church,

should be done with understanding and feeling. Is your faith and the grace of the Holy Spirit burning in your heart as brightly as the flame of the candle you are offering? When you are venerating an icon, do you realize that you yourself are a living icon created in the image and likeness of God, and how God's love and goodness should shine through you? Such thoughts help to prepare you for the Liturgy. But even before reaching the Church, as you leave your home, your thoughts should turn to Christ whom you will seek personally to meet in the Liturgy. The late Father Alexander Schmemann, Dean of St. Vladimir's Seminary, was fond of saying that the journey of the Liturgy begins as you leave home for the Liturgy. More broadly, your life of prayer and your whole attitude toward God and the Liturgy are important aspects of your preparation for the Liturgy. To quote Seminarian Joseph Strzelecki from the video:

> It's an attitude thing. Oftentimes you see people come in late for Church. They come in quickly. Their minds aren't with it. And I think it's very important that we collect our thoughts together, come into Church from the very beginning, be attentive to the words and realize what's happening, that it's a very deep experience of God.

That comment contains a ton of truth about the importance of personal preparation for all of us as we go to the Liturgy. (Note: For more on attitudes to the Liturgy, see Chapter 4).

Active Participation in the Liturgy

Half-way through the first part of the video Father Alkiviadis Calivas, Dean of Hellenic College and Holy Cross, challenged and probably startled his students (and indirectly the video viewers) with some intense, sharp questions about active participation in the Liturgy. "What does it *mean*," he shouted, "to *participate* in the Liturgy? Is it just to go and sing some songs or just to stand there and be there?...What does it *mean* to *you?*"

It is good for us to be startled into full awareness about active participation in the Liturgy. Along with preparation for the Liturgy, active participation is the second key, perhaps even more important than preparation, which helps us to unlock the treasure of the Liturgy and be transformed by beholding the jewel which is Christ. The word "active" in front of the word "participation" is not redundant but must be emphasized time and again because all too often the reality is *passive* participation. Orthodox worshippers seem to be lulled into liturgical passivity by the very process of the ritual drama carried out by the priest and choir or chanter. Although physically awake, many seem liturgically asleep, that is, allowing the music and prayers to roll over their consciousness without any impact. This is why many an Orthodox feel or complain aloud, "I don't get anything out of the Liturgy," and they leave the Liturgy much as they came, without any significant spiritual change.

Do you participate actively in the Divine Liturgy? If yes, how do you do it? If no, what do you think is the problem? What did the video tell you about participation? For one thing, according to the video, we should come to the Liturgy not as spectators but as intimate participants. The Liturgy is not, as Seminarian Paul Tallagan remarked, "a stage production." It is a fervent prayer, a conscious act of worship of the living God. The very word "Liturgy" (*Leitourgia*) means "work of the people," implying meaningful and active participation in the worship of God. Student Eleni Baker hit the mark when she said:

> The Liturgy is really work...not just something you go and observe;...you need to put your whole self into it, to listen, to be aware of nuances and things going on; and then...really try to pay attention.

We must go to the Liturgy ready to do spiritual work. And no one else can do our work for us. If I don't do my work, my part, in the Liturgy, then, for me, it remains undone. I have gone to Church for nothing.

The Liturgy itself is so formulated as to encourage maximum participation. Those featured in the video made many comments about how the Liturgy invites active participation. The Liturgy is in the form of a dialogue between, on the one hand, the priest who often invites us "Let us pray to the Lord" and, on the other hand, the congregation which is supposed to respond continuously "Lord, have mercy." Almost all liturgical petitions, hymns, and prayers are offered in the first person plural. "Let *us* pray to the Lord." "Save *us*, O Son of God." This means that all worshippers, both priest and congregation, are addressing God; they are engaged in a greater dialogue of prayer with God, offering the Liturgy to Him in common. To quote Father Calivas from the video: "The celebration of the Divine Liturgy for us Orthodox is a corporate action of the whole people of God, clergy and laity together."

Of course there are distractions. Our minds fly to different concerns and places. Seminarian Joseph Strzelecki pointed out that we are not always aware that the Liturgy is a continuation of Pentecost; we are looking at the hat on the woman in front of us. These things happen on a human level. But this is why, Father Calivas answers, the Liturgy makes so many calls to attention: "Let us be attentive!" "Wisdom!" "Let us stand!" "Guard the doors!" "Peace be with you!" All these acclamations call us back to full attention and active participation. Furthermore, the Liturgy involves our bodies as well as minds, engaging the participation of the whole person. Seminarian Savas Zembillas described the Liturgy as "embodied prayer;" prayer which "involves our sense of sight and smell and hearing and touch and taste, without belittling any of these."

In the end, active participation depends on our willingness to pray sincerely to God. The work of the Liturgy for each of us is the work of prayer. It is not a question of simply *following* the Liturgy but *praying* the Liturgy— praying the petitions, praying the responses, praying the hymns, praying everything in the Liturgy consciously and from the heart. And prayer, as Seminarian Paul Talagan admitted, does not come easy: It can be hard work. We have to "make an active, conscious effort to pray and worship."

Only by working at praying the Liturgy can we be there consciously in an "active presence." To avoid being passive, "cold spectators," as Seminarian Elias Bouboutsis also remarked, we must come to the Liturgy with open minds and prayerful hearts, realizing that in our lives we need God and that we are creatures dependent on our Creator.

Moreover, if we truly appreciate God's blessings upon us and what He has done for us in Christ, we would take up the work of prayer motivated not only by need but above all by love and gratitude. We sing the Liturgy as a joyous song of faith. The highest expression of Orthodoxy (*orthodoxia*, meaning true worship as well as true faith) is, as the video pointed out, doxology— glorification, praise, and thanksgiving to God, imaging the eternal Liturgy celebrated by the angels in heaven.

(Note: You can read more about active participation in Chapter 4).

Thus far we have talked about the meaning of the Liturgy, preparing for the Liturgy, and participating actively in the Liturgy. We have also touched on some of the contents of the Liturgy. A study of the structure and specific contents of the Liturgy is a big task requiring many sessions. Here we can highlight the main points of the first part of the Liturgy, the Liturgy of the Word, which we have viewed by means of our video program. But before we can even do that, a few more words are necessary about the Service of the Preparation of the Gifts (*Proskomide*, meaning offering or preparation) which we mentioned earlier.[1]

In the video the Proskomide Service is called *Prothesis* (meaning presentation or preparation), the same word used for the side altar table on which the gifts of bread and wine are prepared. A good way of focusing on the content and meaning of the Proskomide Service is to have before you a *prosforon*, the offering bread or specially baked loaf which is marked by a great seal and from which appropriate pieces are lifted as the eucharistic gifts are being prepared. A whole session can be taken up going through a Proskomide Service and talking about it. As you saw in the video, the central piece in the imprinted seal, marked by a cross and bearing the inscription "Jesus Christ conquers," is lifted in commemoration of Christ and is the portion consecrated during the Liturgy as the body of Christ. Many other pieces are lifted up and placed on the paten or small raised tray in commemoration of the Theotokos, the angels, prophets, apostles, many saints,

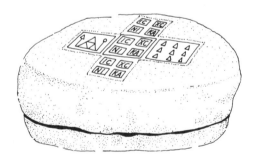

[1] The Proskomide Service has recently been published in Greek and English by Holy Cross Press, 50 Goddard Ave., Brookline, MA 02146

and all other members of the Church, ordained and lay, living and dead.

When this action is completed the paten presents an image of the entire Holy, Catholic, and Apostolic Church gathered around Christ. The whole loaf itself symbolizes the unity of the assembled Church in Christ. During the Proskomide, wine and water are also poured into the chalice at the appropriate time. All these actions are accompanied by short but profound prayers reflecting the themes of the birth and passion of Christ. Then the prepared gifts are covered, ready to be taken in procession during the Great Entrance from the side altar table (the *Prothesis*) to the Holy Altar Table for consecration.

It should also be noted that, historically, the Preparation of the Gifts was originally part of the second part of the Liturgy, the Eucharist, and was done publicly. The people themselves brought the gifts of bread and wine and the deacon(s) presented them to the celebrating priest. However, this liturgical act was eventually elaborated as a service in its own right and was separated from the Eucharist. It could only then find its place at the present location prior to the Liturgy, and conducted privately by the priest, a significant loss in terms of congregational participation in the presentation of the gifts.

We turn now to the first part of the Liturgy, the Liturgy of the Word, which we have seen in the video. This part has sometimes been called the Liturgy of the Catechumens (those being instructed in the faith) because in ancient times unbaptized Christians, unable to partake of Holy Communion, were allowed to participate only in this first part of the Liturgy. The more proper titles, however, are Liturgy of the Word or *Synaxis* (meaning gathering of the people), titles which are derived from the central acts of this service, namely, the reading of the Word of God, which is Scripture, and the sermon. The essential meaning of the Liturgy of the Word, therefore, as the very title indicates, is the gathering of the people of God to hear God's Word proclaimed, interpreted, and applied. The historical origins of this service go back to the days of Jesus and to the worship of the Synagogue which, unlike the Temple, had no sacrifices, but only prayers, the reading of Scripture, and a homily (see Lk. 4:16-21). The public reading of Scripture and the homily became key parts of Christian worship, too, combined with the celebration of the Eucharist.

Do you recognize the significance of the Liturgy of the Word? Do you understand the implications of coming late to the Liturgy and perhaps even missing the Church's public reading of the Holy Scripture? In the Liturgy we receive Christ in two ways. We receive Him through Holy Communion as the sacramental bread of life. We also receive Him through the hearing of God's Word as the spiritual bread of life. This is why before and after the reading of the Gospel we sing: "Glory to You, O Lord, glory to You!" In both of these ways we receive the same Christ who is the true Word of God (*Logos Theou*).

Those who are habitual latecomers to the Liturgy, therefore, miss out on an essential part of the Liturgy. When the Epistle and Gospel lessons are read publicly, they are not there to receive Christ, His teachings, and the truths of God's Word as spiritual food. By their lateness or absence, they also show, without realizing it, that they are not part of the gathering of the people of God ready and eager to hear God's Word. These are offenses against both Christ and His Church, very serious sins of omission, which a thoughtful Christian cannot permit himself or herself to continue.

As the Liturgy of the Word developed in Christian tradition, other liturgical acts, hymns, prayers, and petitions were added to the reading and preaching of the Word of God. In its present form the Liturgy of the Word may be outlined as follows:

Doxological Invocation ("Blessed is the Kingdom")
Great Litany
Antiphons
Small Entrance
Trisagion
Biblical Readings
Sermon

Doxological Invocation

The doxological invocation ("Blessed is the Kingdom") is a confessional praise of the Kingdom of the Holy Trinity, the Father, the Son, and the Holy Spirit.

By saying "Amen" (literally, "let it be so") we all confess and praise the Triune God as King reigning with His majesty, power, and glory over all creation. God's Kingdom is His active reign, ruling power, or lordship, which we acknowledge and glorify, the same Kingdom manifested in the Liturgy and in the new quality of our lives as Christians.

To invoke and praise God's Kingdom is to confess that we are citizens of this Kingdom sharing in all its blessings and righteousness. If God is our King, then He governs our lives. "Who is this God?" asks Bishop Augoustinos in this book.[2] All religions have a God or gods. But our God is the living and personal God of Abraham, Isaac, and Jacob, who revealed Himself through the Prophets and supremely in Christ. This is the God who has spoken to us and whom we know as a righteous, forgiving, and loving Father. "But which people does He govern?" again Bishop Augoustinos asks. He answers: "Those who believe in Him, the true God, and do His will as do the holy angels. God reigns in the hearts of His elect subjects." Blessed be His Kingdom forever!

Great Litany

The Great Litany, sometimes also called Petitions of Peace (*Eirinika*), are a series of one line prayers beseeching God for His spiritual and material blessings covering our entire lives. They include prayers for ordained and civil leaders, as well as for the well-being of the Churches and all people of the world. They end with a remembrance of the example of the Theotokos and Saints, a commitment of our lives to Christ, and a concluding doxology to the Holy Trinity. (The petitions of the Great Litany can be outlined and discussed one by one in an extended study of the Liturgy by a study group with great benefit. In this regard Bishop Augoustinos' work on the Liturgy fills a great gap and is invaluable.) As you study and hear these petitions remember, above all, that they are intended as prayers. You are called to pray by each petition. Pray them, then, to the Lord!

---

[2]*On the Divine Liturgy*, Vol. 1, p. 31.

Antiphons

The Antiphons, three in all and separated by brief petitions, were originally selected series of psalms chanted antiphonally, that is, by two alternating groups of people verse by verse. To these psalms eventually were added hymns to Christ which came to prevail and to displace the psalms. For the sake of brevity we now hear only a few verses from the psalms, if any at all, introducing the hymns to Christ. These hymns, which are "Tes Presvies" ("By the Intercessions of the Theotokos"), "Soson Imas" ("Save Us, O Son of God"), and "O Monogenis Ios" ("Only Begotten Son"), have rich content for study and meditation. In particular the hymn "O Monogenis Ios" is a very ancient hymn proclaiming the Church's doctrine of Christ.

Small Entrance

After the Third Antiphon, there takes place the procession of the Holy Gospel Book called Small Entrance, as compared to the procession of the prepared gifts of bread and wine during the Eucharist called Great Entrance. The Small Entrance, as the video pointed out, is a liturgical way of highlighting the importance of God's Word and symbolizes Christ's coming into the world to teach us God's truth. It is an act drawing attention to and preparing for the readings of the biblical lessons. The Small Entrance is accompanied by hymns called Apolitikia and Kontakia which are resurrectional and/or are related to the feast being celebrated or to the patron Saint of the local Church.

Trisagion

The Trisagion hymn is also a very ancient trinitarian hymn. Its inspiration and content are based on the Old Testament, that is, the prophet Isaiah's vision of God sitting on His throne of glory and surrounded by angelic beings, singing: "Holy, holy, holy is the Lord of hosts; the whole earth is full of His glory" (Is. 6:5). Overwhelmed by this vision of the holiness and majesty of God, Isaiah experienced deeply his own sinfulness, and was then cleansed as an angel touched his lips with a burning coal. Ours should be a similar experience of awe before the holiness and glory of the Lord. The Liturgy is God's throne of majesty, a burning bush shining with God's glory. How can we come before the

Triune God, Father, Son, and Holy Spirit, and sing as do the angels, "Holy God, Holy Mighty, Holy Immortal," if not with hearts filled with awe and divine fire?

Sermon

We have already commented above on the importance of the reading of God's Word taken from the Gospels and Epistles or Book of Acts. In Scripture the Word of God is called "the sword of the Spirit" (Eph. 6:17), "living and active, sharper than any two-edged sword, piercing to the division of soul and spirit" (Heb. 4:12). But how about the sermon, the preaching of the Word of God? Here is how Bishop Augoustinos describes the importance of preaching for the establishment of the Churches in history:

> Not one Church was established without sacred preaching, and no Church thrived or multiplied its membership without preaching. In subterranean cemeteries called catacombs, where Christians took refuge in times of persecution, there was always a sermon when the Divine Liturgy was offered. It was a simple preaching which came from the heart of the bishop or priest.[3]

The sermon is an integral part to the reading of the biblical lessons and should reflect the truth and power of God's Word. If God's Word is a sword, then the preaching of God's Word, the sermon, cannot be a limp and dull instrument. The sermon often loses effectiveness if it merely presents the preacher's own ideas, relies on his skills, or is based on general philosophical and moralistic thinking. If it is to be a vehicle of God's Word, then the sermon must be preached from the heart and in the spirit of God's Word. The sermon will indeed reflect the creative energy of God's Word when the preacher: (a) truly preaches the good news of salvation; (b) develops Christ-centered sermons; (c) relies on the Holy Spirit and the authority of God's Word; (d) prepares well and consistently, and (e) delivers the sermon with living faith.

---

[3]*Ibid.*, p. 231

Also, it must strongly be said that the sermon belongs after the reading of God's Word, not at the end of the Liturgy! No excuses can justify dislocating the preached word from its proper structural and theological place in the Liturgy of the Word. Otherwise the Liturgy of the Word remains incomplete. The value and power of a crucial liturgical tradition is lost by neglect and by unhelpful accommodation. Therefore, every necessary measure must be taken, including adequate notification to worshippers, arranging to hold latecomers in the narthex, and a prayerful substantial sermon, to make sure the the good news of God's Word resounds in our Churches in the proper way and at the proper times.

We conclude our brief review of the contents of the Liturgy of the Word by pointing to the mystical or silent prayers. Anyone who closely follows the movement of the Liturgy with a Liturgy book will notice the many prayers throughout the Liturgy intended to be read with a quiet voice by the priests. These prayers are gems! They are more than worthy of devoted attention and meditation. Almost all of them are also cast in the first person plural inviting the whole congregation's attention and participation. As much as possible, listen attentively to these prayers, learn to eye-read them if you cannot hear them, and above all silently pray them as the priest offers them to God on your behalf.

At the beginning of the video the narrator connected the Liturgy with daily life. He said:

> The very word Liturgy, or *Leitourgia*, means "work of the people," that is, the worship and glorification of God through meaningful and active participation in the Divine Liturgy *and through daily life and witness.*

The Liturgy is intimately connected to life. The Liturgy is communion with God, true life with God, which intends to touch and transform all aspects of our personal, family, and social lives. The Liturgy is not an escape, but a spiritual retreat from ordinary life, for a return to and for the renewal of all life. In its future vision the Liturgy looks to the fulness of the coming Kingdom and the transfiguration of the whole cosmos. The Divine Liturgy, therefore, unites all of time, past, present, and future, and embraces all things, human beings, physical and spiritual needs, social and ecological values. It applies supremely to all reality, seen and unseen, which it seeks to transform by the light of the transfiguration of the Lord.

Thinking about the video or your own knowledge of the Liturgy what are some applications of the Liturgy to life? The petitions of the Great Litany have to do with many aspects of our daily concerns including peace among nations, good weather, safe travel, and help in sickness or suffering. The gold or silver plated Gospel Book, as the video pointed out, symbolizes the treasure of life, the value of Christ's teachings as spiritual food for our daily lives. "The words of Christ and the Apostles," said the narrator, "are to be applied daily by us in the times and circumstances in which we live." The Seminarian who chanted the Epistle reminded us of St. Paul's words, "the fruit of the Spirit is love, joy, peace, patience, kindness...," and also of his exhortation, "Bear one another's burdens and so fulfill the law of Christ." All these things have very much to do with life and with concrete applications of the Liturgy to everyday living.

One can say that the Liturgy is not truly a Liturgy unless it is indeed applied, unless it impacts on our daily life. When we invoke and glorify God's Kingdom, we can meditate on ways in which God is our King and how we show it in our daily decisions. When we call to mind the Theotokos and the Saints, we can think about our own examples of love for and obedience to God. When we sing, "Glory to You, O Lord, glory to You," we must ask how we glorify Him by the witness of our daily conduct. When we receive Christ through Holy Communion, we must remember that He lives in us daily. Approach the Liturgy in this spirit. Seek yourself to make connections between the Liturgy and your daily life. You will be amazed at the discoveries you will make by the help of the Holy Spirit.

As the preacher in the video said: "The Liturgy is a sacred moment in which Christ, our risen Lord, comes in our midst...that *our whole life may be a liturgy to Him*." There is a liturgy after the Liturgy! There is a *liturgy in life*, as well as a *Liturgy in the Church*. In both, Christ is the chief Celebrant, working in and through us. The same words He addressed to the disciples in the Gospel lesson we heard in the video, He also speaks to us: "Peace be with you. As the Father has sent me, even so I send you...Receive the Holy Spirit" (Jn 20:21-22). Christ empowers us through the Liturgy to continue His mission in the world and to be His witnesses in the ordinary circumstances of private life, home, work, civic duty, and play. The connection between the Liturgy in the Church and the liturgy in ordinary life is captured by the following mystical prayer offered to Christ just before the reading of the Gospel:

> Shine within our hearts, loving Master, the pure light of Your divine knowledge and open the eyes of our minds that we may comprehend the message of Your Gospel. Instill in us also reverence for Your blessed commandments, so that having conquered sinful desires, we may pursue a spiritual way of life, thinking and doing all those things that are pleasing to You. For You, Christ our God, are the light of our souls and bodies, and to You we give glory, together with Your Father...and Your...Spirit, now and forever and to the ages of ages. Amen.

3

THE EUCHARIST

The second part of the Divine Liturgy is the Eucharist (*Eucharistia*) which means "Thanksgiving." This title comes from the very actions of Jesus at the Last Supper. Jesus broke the bread and offered the cup after "having given thanks" (*eucharistesas*) to His Father in heaven (Lk. 22:17-19). So we, too, through the Liturgy, give thanks to God for the gift of His Son and all His blessings. Just before the consecration of the gifts of bread and wine, the priest invites the congregation: "Let us give thanks to the Lord." A most profound prayer of thanksgiving follows while the hymn "Se Imnoumen" is sung by the choir and congregation: "We praise You, we bless You, we give thanks to You...Lord our God." At other times in the Liturgy, as well, we give thanks to the Holy Trinity. One could say that we Orthodox have a Thanksgiving Day each time the Divine Liturgy is celebrated.

But there is also another more recent title for the second part of the Liturgy, that is, Liturgy of the Faithful. This title as the video explained, echoes an ancient tradition, no longer in practice, by which the *catechumens* (Christians being instructed in the faith who were unbaptized and therefore unable to receive Holy Communion) left at the end of the Liturgy of the Word. Their departure was signaled by the call: "All you who are catechumens depart...let no catechumen remain. All you who are faithful, let us again pray to the Lord." Then the solemn rite of the Eucharist continued in the presence of the baptized faithful alone. Appropriate prayers were also offered for both the catechumens and the faithful.

Although for the sake of brevity these liturgical actions and prayers are no longer practiced in our parishes, they are part of the full text of the Liturgy and remind us of the special commitment the Christian faithful, baptized Orthodox Christians, bear by virtue of their baptism. The prayers remind us, as well, that we are saved through faith and of St. Paul's words: "For by grace you have been saved through faith;...this is not your own doing, it is the gift of God" (Eph. 2:8).

Having heard the explanations of the video what, would you say, is the essence of the Eucharist? What were the highlights or most inspiring moments of the Eucharist for you? Why do we need to celebrate the Eucharist with special care and concentration? What are the main parts of the Eucharist? Do you have any questions about what you saw and heard in the video? How do you relate the Eucharist to daily life? Is the Eucharist truly a thanksgiving for you? For what things are you thankful to God? In what various ways can we express our gratitude to God? How is it possible, in St. Paul's words, to "give thanks in all *circumstances*" (1 Thess. 5:18)? (Note to study leader or facilitator: if the time schedule is short, proceed with discussion on the basis of the above and similar questions; if the time schedule is longer, see pp. 92–93 of this Study Guide for further instructions on how to use what follows in this chapter.)

We have said that the Liturgy is a celebration of the life of Christ. Through the Liturgy we both remember and re-live the ministry and saving work of Christ. In the Proskomide or Preparation of the Gifts Christ comes to us as the Holy Child of Bethlehem. In the Liturgy of the Word Christ comes to us as Teacher. In the Liturgy of the Faithful or the Eucharist Christ comes to us as the Archpriest who has once for all offered Himself on the Cross for the redemption of the world. The solemnity of the Eucharist lies in the re-living of the awesome sacrifice of Christ by which He conquered the powers of sin, death and Satan.

But the Eucharist also celebrates the resurrection of Christ and the joy of the new creation. Moreover, what can be both more solemn and more joyous simultaneously, than the presence of our beloved Savior in our midst, the Bridegroom of the Church, with whom we are united through Holy Communion? St. Ephraem lyrically speaks of the Eucharist as another wedding feast in Cana, Christ's own spiritual marriage festival to which He invites His bride— the Church at one level, the soul at another.[1] Therefore, awe, wonder, praise, and joy, harmoniously united, are the marks of the Eucharist.

In what follows we are going to highlight the Eucharist in terms of (1) the Great Entrance; (2) the Offering of the Gifts (*Anaphora*); (3) the Lord's Prayer; (4) Holy Communion, and (5) the Dismissal Blessing. As we meditate on these significant parts of the Eucharist, we

[1]For an excellent sample of the hymns and poems of St. Ephraem, see Sebastian Brock, *The Harp of the Spirit* (St. Alban and St. Sergius, 1983) from whom this reference is taken (p. 18).

want to consider both their spiritual meaning and their daily application in our lives.

When kings were ready to enter a city, heralds were sent ahead to announce their coming. People rushed out to the gates and streets to welcome them with banners and shouts of joy. Today when leaders of nations make state visits and formal appearances, they, too, are greeted with cheers and flags. In the Great Entrance Christ Himself, as the High Priest of the Church, comes to us in procession on His way to the Cross. This is the symbolic meaning of the Great Entrance. How should we welcome Him? In his book *Living the Liturgy*, Father Stanley Harakas writes:

> When the Great Entrance takes place, Christ is bearing His Cross for us, in our mind's eye. We are part of the crowd on the *via Dolorosa*, the "way of sorrows" which Christ travelled as He went to His crucifixion. We deliberately "put away all worldly care." We open our hearts that "we may receive the King of all" as He comes into *our* world to die for us. What would you have felt in your heart if you had been there then? Unworthiness? Wonder? Love? Gratitude? All these are appropriate responses at this moment of liturgical action.[2]

The Great Entrance is the first important liturgical act of the Eucharist. Originally it was a much less

[2]Stanley S. Harakas, *Living the Liturgy* (Light and Life, 1974), p. 95.

dramatic transfer of the gifts of bread and wine from a side table in the Church to the Holy Table in the altar by the deacons in order to be consecrated. This was and still remains the practical purpose of the procession which was gradually highly dramatized in comparison with the Small Entrance featuring the procession of the Gospel. The two entrances should, however, not be seen as one being greater than the other in spiritual meaning. In both we receive the same Christ, as Teacher in the first and as High Priest in the second. Nor is it proper to kneel during the Great Entrance because, unlike in the case of the Pre-Sanctified Liturgy, the precious gifts are not yet consecrated but only dedicated to Christ (during the Service of the Preparation of the Gifts). It may also be noted that the Great Entrance is preceded by a Great Litany, as well as prayers for the catechumens and the faithful, no longer usually recited in parishes, but acting as transitions between the Liturgy of the Word and the Eucharist. These prayers and the Great Litany could be studied specifically for their own value.

The spiritual meaning of the Great Entrance is superbly expressed by the Cherubic Hymn:

> We who mystically represent the Cherubim sing the thrice holy hymn to the life giving Trinity. Let us set aside all the cares of life that we may receive the King of all invisibly escorted by the angelic hosts. Alleluia. Alleluia. Alleluia.

What an awesome moment! The Lord of lords and the King of kings is mystically in our midst. He comes humbly in the form of bread and wine. He comes to offer His sacrifice for our salvation. But angels invisibly escort Him. Think of the acolytes as symbolizing the escorting angels. You and I, too, join them. We become part of this spiritual event in welcoming Christ the King. We are like the angelic beings in Isaiah's vision singing to God the thrice holy hymn: "Holy, holy, holy!" We represent the Cherubim before the glory of the throne of God calling to one another: "Alleluia!" "Praise the Lord!"

How can one remain unmoved and with a cold heart at moments such as these! When one begins truly to understand the Liturgy not as a rite of ritual but as a spiritual event, then he or she is likely to agree with what student Georgia Mandakas said in the video: "I am just awed by what goes on. And I try to share that with my friends...It's hard for them to understand...Well, come and see!"

While the Cherubic hymn is being sung, the priest offers a stirring personal prayer to the Lord of all, the King of glory, whom no one bound by worldly desires can worthily serve. Only by God's love and mercy can one approach the mystery of the Eucharist. The priest humbly asks for the Lord's forgiveness and empowerment to stand before the Holy Table and offer the Eucharist. He acknowledges that Christ Himself is the true Celebrant of the Eucharist, "the Offerer and the Offered" (Gift), to whom belongs all the glory. The priest then censes the Holy Table, the Prothesis Table, the icons of the iconostas, and all the people while reciting the 51st Psalm (LXX 50), a moving psalm about God's mercy, forgiveness, and renewal.

Incense itself symbolizes a spiritual offering to God, the rising of prayer before God's throne (Psalm 141:2). Pure incense is the tear of aromatic trees in Lebanon which are incised to produce it. We can liken faithful Christians to aromatic trees spreading the aroma of faith and virtue in the world; and often they are cut, passing through pain and suffering, in order to yield the sweet scent of grace.[3] After all these actions, the priest, with awe and fear of God, lifts up the precious gifts and carries them in the procession of the Great Entrance.

What are your feelings and thoughts during the Great Entrance? What should the disposition and action of the congregation be? We are called to set aside all earthly cares in order to receive Christ as our personal Lord and King. Our work is to pray and to say inwardly: "Yes, Lord, You are my King!" But it is not easy to set aside our mundane concerns. The mind, so the Desert Fathers used to say, is like a wagonful of monkeys. The seminary classroom discussion in the video pointed out that there is a tension between the stillness of concentrated prayer and the turmoil of daily cares, just as there is a tension between the spiritual energy required by the Liturgy and the relaxation of the weekend as expected by modern culture.

[3]Augoustinos Kantiotes, *On the Divine Liturgy*, Vol. 2, pp. 52-53.

What is one to do? The tension will not go away. We are faced with choices and commitments. The Liturgy, as well as life, are matters of choices and commitment. Once we make them, we strive to be true to them with God's help. In the Liturgy, we can bring to God our earthly concerns; and this we do through many petitions. But our main purpose is to make room in our hearts and minds for Christ. The Liturgy is the Lord's time. If Christ appears and speaks to us, as we believe He does, through the Liturgy, then all our attention should be directed to Him. There come moments when everything inside of ourselves must be silent; only Christ must be seen and heard.[4] When this miracle occurs, then we know that the Liturgy itself can be a refreshing vacation from the hustle and bustle of life, a Christian "R and R"–refreshment and renewal which help us to see more clearly and to carry out more effectively our daily tasks.

In the Great Entrance the precious gifts of bread and wine, dedicated to Christ, are brought from the Prothesis Table to the Holy Table for consecration later in the Liturgy.[5] In the Old Testament "the first fruits of the earth," figs, grapes, lambs and other, were offered to God. We offer bread and wine. These gifts are fruits of the earth but they also require human labor and cooperation for the wheat to become bread and the grapes to become wine. In like manner our own cooperation is needed for our salvation. God wants us to be saved and offers everything for our salvation. But to receive God's gift of salvation He requires our sincere efforts and cooperation in terms of our inward spiritual attention, positive choices, clear commitment, the work of prayer, and virtuous living.

Moreover, the Lord, to whom we bring bread and wine, is ready to return infinitely superior spiritual gifts. To the disciples, whom He called to leave off fishing, He promised a new calling as fishers of men and women. To those who labor and carry heavy burdens, whom He invited to come to Him, He promised true rest and peace. To us who bring to Him bread and wine in the Liturgy, whom He commanded to continue the Eucharist in remembrance of Him, He gives Himself as

[4]*Ibid.*, p. 42.
[5]The thoughts which follow are taken from Augoustinos Kantiotes, *On the Divine Liturgy*, Vol. 2, pp. 64-71.

the heavenly bread. We remember Him in the Liturgy. We pray that He will remember us in His glorious Kingdom. And so the priest chants during the great Entrance: "May the Lord, our God, remember all of you (or us) in His kingdom, now and forever and to the ages of ages."

*The
Offering
of
the
Gifts
(Anaphora)*

The heart of the Eucharist is the offering and consecration of the eucharistic gifts. This liturgical act goes back to Jesus Himself at the Last Supper. It is the oldest part of the Eucharist as celebrated by the ancient Church. As the rite of the Eucharist developed historically, however, other preparatory elements were added to it: (a) Petitions known as *Plerotika*, (b) the kiss of peace, and (c) the Nicene Creed.

The name *Plerotika* (Completing Petitions) derives from the verb *plerosomen* of the first petition: "Let us complete our prayer to the Lord." These are prayers of requests for God's guidance and protection in life, His forgiveness and peace, His material and spiritual blessings, until the coming of the Kingdom. The tone set by these petitions is that the purity of the gifts should be accompanied by the purity of our lives.[6] The great mystery of the Eucharist about to take place requires repentant hearts free of evil, anger, and resentments, so that the gifts may be offered worthily. As we pray "for the precious gifts here presented," we also pray for holiness in life. These petitions end with a mystical prayer to God Almighty, who alone is holy, to accept the gifts and spiritual sacrifices of the priests and the lay faithful.

The kiss of peace is signalled by the priest's call: "Let us love one another that with one mind we may confess." These words echo Christ's command to mutual love among His followers (Jn 13:34-35). At this point the early Christians exchanged the kiss of peace, now usually exchanged only by concelebrating priests, a sign of reconciliation before the Offering of the Gifts. Here is how St. Cyril of Jerusalem explains the spiritual meaning of this kiss as a holy kiss:

> You must not suppose that this kiss
> is the kiss ordinarily exchanged in the
> streets by ordinary friends. This kiss is

[6]Kantiotes, Vol. 2, p. 75.

different, for it effects a commingling of souls, and pledges complete forgiveness. The kiss, then, is a sign of a true union of hearts, and of banishing any grudge. On account of this Christ said: "...Go first to be reconciled with your brother, and then come back and offer your gift" (Mt. 5:24). The kiss, then, is a reconciliation and is, therefore, holy, as the blessed Paul declared somewhere, saying "Greet one another with a holy kiss" (Rm 16:16; 1 Cor. 16:20).[7]

The Nicene Creed is a confession of the Orthodox Faith centered on the Holy Trinity. The earlier call to mutual love was followed by a call to confess the Holy Trinity, "Father, Son, and Holy Spirit, Trinity one in essence and inseparable." It can be said that the trinitarian dogma is the foundation of the Christian Faith. Just as we Christians, when speaking about love, call to mind a specific kind of love, the spiritual and sacrificial love of Christ, so also, when we speak about God, we should call to mind the living God of Scripture, Father, Son, and Holy Spirit.

Faith and life are closely related. We are not talking about must any kind of love or any kind of god, but the love of God the Father expressed through Jesus Christ, the Son, and by the power of the Holy Spirit. The life of Christians needs to reflect the quality of life and the mutual love of the Trinity. This is why we recite the Nicene Creed, the full statement of the trinitarian faith. We believe in God the Father, Creator of heaven and earth, and of all things visible and invisible. We believe in one Lord, Jesus Christ, the Son of God, true God, incarnate, crucified under Pontius Pilate, risen, ascended, glorified, and One who will return in glory at the time of the final resurrection. We also believe in the Holy Spirit, the Lord and Giver of life, who inspired the prophets and apostles, who is present in the One, Holy, Catholic, and Apostolic Church, and whose grace we receive at baptism. The Creed, too, we would remember, is a prayer, a living testimony to the truth of the Orthodox Faith. When we recite it, the video narrator

[7]Quoted by Daniel J. Sheerin, *The Eucharist: Message of the Fathers of the Church* (Michael Glazier, 1986), p. 68.

observed, we "recite it as a personal commitment to that truth to be fulfilled in daily living."

Having confessed the essence of our faith, we make ready to celebrate the heart of the Eucharist, the Holy *Anaphora* or Holy Offering. The most solemn moment has arrived. "Let us stand well," the priest bids the congregation. "Let us stand in awe. Let us be attentive, that we may present the holy offering in peace." Have you noticed the icon of the Last Supper above the royal doors of the altar in Orthodox Churches? At this moment you, too, are invited to enter the upper room and to join the company of Jesus and the apostles. You, too, spiritually and symbolically, become a participant in the first Eucharist, witnessing the actions and words of Jesus as He broke the bread and offered the cup. No higher honor on earth exists. No greater privilege can be bestowed on anyone. The Lord invites you to gather around His table of love for the mystery of the Eucharist.

What should your feelings and thoughts be at this moment? "Mercy and peace, a sacrifice of praise." Let your own thoughts be on God's great mercy. Let your own heart be filled with God's peace. Let your own lips offer a sacrifice of praise. Allow your whole self to enter into the Eucharist with full awareness and active participation. When the priest blesses you with the apostolic blessing, "The grace of our Lord Jesus Christ, and the love of God the Father, and the communion of the Holy Spirit, be with all of you" (2 Cor. 13:14), consciously return the blessing to him with the words, "And with your spirit." When the priest invites the congregation,"Let us lift up our hearts," truly lift up

your heart to heaven, casting aside all mundane concerns. When the priest asks, "Let us give thanks to the Lord," truly give your thanks to the Lord for all His blessings and for the Eucharist being celebrated. In doing so, you, too, become part of the mystical event of the Last Supper as it unfolds before you in the Liturgy.

The Offering of the Gifts takes place through the great Eucharistic Prayer. The great Eucharistic Prayer begins with the words, "It is proper and right to sing to You, bless You, praise You, thank You..." and ends with another blessing by the priest: "The mercy of our great God and Savior Jesus Christ be with all of you." The great Eucharistic Prayer includes a number of liturgical acts and appears to be interrupted by several hymns. However, it is one continuous prayer, a single magnificent liturgical unit within the Eucharist. Its component parts may briefly be outlined as follows:

(a) Thanksgiving—We thank God the Father for His nature and greatness, His creative and redeeming work, as well as His material and spiritual blessings, including the Liturgy being celebrated.

(b) The Trisagion—We sing "the victory hymn" in glorification of God, "Holy, holy, holy, Lord Sabaoth, heaven and earth are filled with Your glory," yet another iconic representation of angels and archangels singing around the throne of God (Is. 6:1-3).

(c) The Words of Institution—We remember the night of Christ's holy passion and the Last Supper; and we also hear Christ's words by which He established the Eucharist: "Take, eat; this is my body," and "Drink of it all of you; this is my blood of the new covenant."

(d) Offering of the Gifts—The bread and wine are lifted up as an offering to God with the words, "We offer to You these gifts from Your own gifts in all and for all;" and we follow with the singing of "Se Imnoumen" ("We Praise You").

(e) Epiclesis and Consecration— The celebrant priest invokes God for the coming of the Holy Spirit: "Send down Your Holy Spirit upon us and upon these gifts," that the bread and wine may become the body and blood of Christ by the power of the Spirit.

(f) The Commemorations— In the long ending of the Eucharistic Prayer we commemorate the communion of glorified saints, especially the Theotokos to whom a special hymn of praise is chanted; we commemorate as well the living members of the Church, especially the hierarchs, the civil authorities, those who are suffering or in need, those who do good works or serve in God's vineyard, and also the entire Church and whole world on behalf of which the Liturgy is universally offered.

One of the priests in the video explained that the Eucharistic Prayer "brings us into the context of the Last Supper...We re-enact or, better, re-live, spiritually and mystically, the Last Supper of Christ in which He is our Lord and Master and we are the disciples partaking of that table of love." By means of the Last Supper Jesus acted out the significance of His mission as "the mediator of a new covenant" (Heb. 9:15). He celebrated a new passover and a new exodus through His sacrifice on the Cross, the liberation of humankind from the powers of sin and death.

Think of this moment of the Eucharist as your sacramental participation in the atoning death of Christ which we re-live and proclaim until He comes (1 Cor. 11:26). Think of it as your presence at the foot of the Cross of Christ, your passover from death to life, your exodus from the darkness of sin to the light of the resurrection. Christ loves you. Christ died for you. The crucified and risen Christ speaks to you, saying "Take, eat, this is my body" and "Drink of it...; this is my blood."

Nicholas Cabasilas writes that through the Eucharist God's saving righteousness comes to us and releases us from sin, whereas human righteousness by itself avails nothing.[8] The Eucharistic Prayer anchors itself on the good news of the Gospel when the priest prays to God: "You so loved Your world that You gave Your only begotten Son so that whoever believes in Him should not perish, but have eternal life" (see Jn 3:16). Think of the Eucharist as your good news, your free gift of salvation, your experience of God's saving love and forgiveness in Christ from which neither "height, nor depth, nor anything else in all creation," will be able to separate you (Rom. 8:39).

When the Prophet Elijah was challenged to prove to idolaters that the God of Israel was the true God, He prayed to God to send fire upon the makeshift altar on Mt. Carmel. Immediately, fire fell from heaven and consumed the altar as well as the slaughtered calf on it. Thus the people believed that the God of Elijah was the true God and they said: "The Lord, He is God; the Lord, He is God" (1 Kings 18:22-38). St. John Chrysostom,[9] who mentions this miracle of Elijah, compares it with the greater miracle of the consecration of the eucharistic gifts. However, according to St. John Chrysostom, the priest asks not for the judgmental fire which fell on the altar of Elijah, but for the Holy Spirit whose grace cleanses and illumines us. The Holy Spirit changes the bread and wine into the body and blood of Christ.

The Church Fathers do not speculate about this great mystery. They only draw an analogy between the incarnation and the consecration. As the Spirit fell upon the Virgin Mary and she conceived Christ in her womb, in some like manner the Spirit falls upon the gifts and Christ Himself is present in the consecrated bread and wine. This is a mystical and sacramental change rather than a physical one. As the video narrator noted: "When we receive Holy Communion, we still taste the qualities of bread and wine, but by faith we receive the true body and blood of the Lord, and are united with the glorified human nature of the risen Christ."

What an awesome miracle! What an unspeakable gift! Christ was incarnate and born in a manger. Now He becomes present in the bread and wine and ready to

The Life in Christ, p. 121.

[9]This reference comes from Kantiotes, *On the Divine Liturgy*, Vol. 2, pp. 206-207.

enter into the manger of our unworthy selves. Heaven becomes earth so that earth may become heaven. The consecrated gifts are the "medicine of immortality," the source of many blessings.

According to the Eucharistic Prayer, the eucharistic gifts are "for vigilance of soul, forgiveness of sins, communion of the Holy Spirit, fulfillment of the kingdom of heaven, confidence before God, and not in judgment or condemnation." Through the consecrated gifts we mystically receive Christ Himself as the bread of eternal life. We meet Christ personally and are united with Him in an intimate union beyond human language. Hear the words of Christ from the Gospel of St. John: "He who eats my flesh and drinks my blood abides in me, and I in him...This is the bread which came down from heaven;...He who eats this bread will live for ever" (Jn 6:56,58).

In the words of a hymn, "What shall we give to the Lord in return for all His gifts?"[10] What should our response be to the divine gifts of the Eucharist? The Divine Liturgy itself has the answer: adoration, praise, and thanksgiving. These are the marks of true worship of God."Se Imnoumen...We praise You, we bless You, we give thanks to You, and we pray to You, Lord our God."

In a great prayer of thanksgiving recorded in the First Book of Chronicles (1 Chr. 29:10-19), King David, bearing the gifts of the people for the building of the Temple, prays to God: "But who am I, and what is my people, that we should be able thus to offer (these gifts)? For all things come from You and of Your own have we given You" (1 Chr. 29:14). The Church Fathers chose the same key words from the Old Testament to place in the Eucharistic Prayer at the offering of the bread and wine: "We offer to You these gifts from Your own gifts in all and for all." But in offering these simple fruits of the earth, as the late Father Alexander Schmemann commented so profoundly, we offer to God the totality of ourselves, of our lives, and of the whole world in which we live. We can experience a movement of adoration and praise, a eucharistic ascension in which all joy and suffering, all hunger and satisfaction find their ultimate meaning in Christ's sacrifice which is our Eucha-

---

[10]*Octoechos*, Hymn of Praises, Tone Seven.

rist.[11] It is here that we discover both the essential connection between the Eucharist and life, as well as the cosmic significance of the Eucharist. No more profound commentary on the hymn "Se Imnoumen" can be made than the following words by Father Schmemann:

> We know that we were created as celebrants of the sacrament of life, of its transformation into life in God, communion with God. We know that real life is "eucharist," a movement of love and adoration toward God, the movement in which alone the meaning and the value of all that exists can be revealed and fulfilled.[12]

The Lord's Prayer

Our video program called the Lord's Prayer a link between the Offering of the Gifts and Holy Communion. Not only the Lord's Prayer but also other petitions and another mystical prayer serve as links or transitions between the consecration and receiving of the eucharistic gifts. In the petitions we pray for the consecrated gifts, the grace of the Holy Spirit, and unity in faith. We also, once more in the Liturgy, "commit ourselves, and one another, and our whole life to Christ our God." This commitment to Christ is further expanded by the mystical prayer that follows in which we entrust to Christ "our whole life and hope," and also ask Him to make us worthy to partake of His heavenly mysteries with a clear conscience. We then ask God the Father to make us worthy to offer to Him the Lord's Prayer.

Although the Lord's Prayer is one of several liturgical links at this part of the Eucharist, it clearly stands out on its own as a highlight of the Liturgy, recited by both the priest and the congregation. The meaning of the Lord's Prayer is summed up by the video narrator with these words:

> A model prayer and a precious pearl which comes from the mouth of Jesus Himself, the Lord's Prayer is a prayer of glorification of God—His name, will,

[11]Alexander Schmemann, *For the Life of the World*, pp. 34-36.
[12]*Ibid.*, p. 34.

and kingdom— and a prayer of petition through which we ask God for daily bread, forgiveness of sins, and strength in times of trial and temptation.

What does the Lord's Prayer mean to you? You may recite it often at meals, as a morning or evening prayer, and at Church. We often say the Lord's Prayer quickly and by rote. Some of us do not pay much attention to what we are actually praying to God, whom we dare address as "Father." Sometimes the Lord's Prayer becomes a prayer of convenience, a quick fix, before a committee meeting or another gathering. A casual attitude such as this is really to our shame. The pearls of the Christian faith should not be treated in this way. Rather, we need to pray the Lord's Prayer unhurriedly and with deliberate care, concentrating on each word and on the meaning of each of its petitions. The Church Fathers help us to rediscover the meaning and power of the Lord's Prayer.[13] (The group leader may skip the following commentary and go to p. 44).

"Our Father who art in heaven"

These are the words of the Son of God who alone enjoys the divine prerogative of calling God "Father." To those who believe in Him, who already possess His blessings by faith and baptism, He has also granted the authority and privilege to address God as "Father." They are sons and daughters of God by grace, reborn of the Spirit, co-heirs with Christ. Let them speak to God the Father with the words of His Son. But let them also lead a life worthy of God, showing the qualities of the Father and the virtues of Christ, so that the Father may walk among them as in a garden.

It is a daring thing to call God, who is absolute goodness, holiness, and love, "Father." You call Him "Father;"

[13]What follows is a brief interpretation of the Lord's Prayer based on John Chrysostom, Gregory of Nyssa, Cyprian, Cyril of Alexandria, Maximus the Confessor, and Origen, all of whom have written commentaries or essays on the Lord's Prayer.

honor Him also with ready obedience, seeking to be perfect as He is perfect, and making your whole life a prayer to Him. Those unrepentant and persistent in evil invoke not the Father in heaven but the Infernal One, the father of lies, whose sons and daughters they are.

Let believers also know— for this is a prayer of believers— that they call God "Father" in common: "*Our* Father...Give *us* this day...Forgive *us our* debts." They belong to one body, united in the Church, praying for one another, looking for each other's good, equal as brothers and sisters before God, whether poor man or king, all sharing the supreme honor of calling God their Father with confidence and purity of conscience. Let them also remember, when they say "in heaven," where their true homeland is and that their true citizenship is not on earth but in heaven.

"Hallowed be Thy name"

A name reflects the identity of one named. God's name is the sacred name of Yahweh, I AM THAT I AM, the Holy One of Israel. God is always holy. How can we pray that His name be hallowed or sanctified? First it can be hallowed in the sense of praise and glorification. The Psalms exalt the name of the Lord: "I will sing praise to the name of the Lord" (Ps. 7:17). "Let us exalt His name together" (Ps. 34:3). "Blessed be His glorious name forever" (Ps. 72:19).

Second, God's name can be hallowed in us and through us. God has commanded: "Be holy, as I am holy" (1 Pt. 1:16). When we lead righteous and holy lives God is glorified. God's name may be either glorified or blasphemed by the way I live. Therefore, when I pray, "Hallowed by Thy name," I also in essence pray, "May I become through Your help blameless, righteous, and holy; may I abstain from every evil, speak the truth, and do justice." I exalt God's name and also pray for my own daily sanctification. In doing so I seek to fulfill Jesus' words: "Let your light so shine before others, that they may see your good works and give glory to your Father in heaven" (Mt. 5:16).

"Thy kingdom come"

God is always King! He reigns for ever. His kingdom is eternal. How then can we pray that His kingdom come? We pray for the actualization and the fullness of His kingdom in our lives, the world, and history. The kingdom can be more visibly manifested in us. The kingdom is experienced within us as an inward spiritual order; and is revealed outside of us as the outward work of virtue and witness. Sin cannot co-exist with the kingdom. To pray for the coming of the kingdom is to pray for the coming of the Holy Spirit who imparts life-giving power, dispelling corruption, freeing us from the shackles of sin, and giving us life, peace, and joy.

Too, we pray that the world which lies in darkness, may acknowledge the living God as King and may be released from the power of the devil's kingdom. Finally, we look to the consummation of the world and the coming of the fullness of God's kingdom, the time of the glorious return of Christ, the universal resurrection, and the judgment. Let us pray and be prepared for these awesome events.

"Thy will be done on earth as it is in heaven"

Jesus at Gethsemane prayed: "My Father, if it be possible, let this cup pass from me; nevertheless, not as I will, but as Thou wilt" (Mt. 26:39). He instructed us, too, in all circumstances, to do God's will. What is God's will? God's will is most perfectly revealed in the teachings and example of Christ. How can we accomplish God's will? First by renouncing what is contrary to God's will. We need to recognize that we are weak; we do not turn from evil to good as easily as we turn to evil. We need a changed heart and God's grace. Then we fulfill God's will by following positively the precepts and example of Christ. The accomplishment of God's will is the health of the soul. If we desire it, nothing can hinder us from perfection by God's help.

"Heaven" symbolizes the obedience of angels. We can make earth a heaven by our obedience. Or "heaven" can symbolize our spirit, the new nature, and "earth" our flesh, the old nature, the two being in conflict with one another. We must let the earthly give way to the heavenly, the works of the flesh give way to the fruit of the Spirit. Again, "heaven" can symbolize the Church which is called to carry on Christ's mission. God's will is that all may be saved. To pray for God's will is thus also to pray for the conversion of the world.

"Give us this day our daily bread"

Jesus taught us not to be anxious about what we shall eat, and what we shall drink, but to seek first the kingdom of God and its righteousness (Mt. 6:31-33). This we do in the Lord's Prayer through the above petitions glorifying God's name, kingdom, and will. But Jesus did not say that we should not ask God for our daily necessities and other personal needs, for He said: "And all these things shall be yours as well" (Mt. 6:33). This we do through the remaining petitions of the Lord's Prayer about daily bread, mutual forgiveness, and protection from evil. When we pray for bread, which represents all the bodily requirements necessary and sufficient for daily living, we cast our care upon the Lord (1 Pt. 5:7). We ask for simplicity of sustenance, not delicacies, riches, and estates; and for bread through just labor, for the bread of the Lord is the fruit of justice.

However, there is also a far greater incorporeal bread, the bread of life, which is Christ Himself. This is the essential bread, the bread which imparts true being, the living bread from heaven. We receive Christ as the bread of life through the Eucharist, the words of Scripture, and virtuous living. We need daily bread, whether simple or spiritual, on each day. Both body and soul need nourishment every day. The past and the future are beyond our grasp. Only the present can we call our own. Human life is but the life of a day under the care of God.

"And forgive our debts (trespasses) as we forgive our debtors (those who trespass against us)"

Forgiveness is the special prerogative of God and the summit of Christian virtue. Nothing makes us so like God, as being ready to forgive our wrong-doers. Of course, we can only forgive wrongs committed against us specifically; we are not lords over all the actions of others.

What is meant by debt? Debt is a sin, a transgression or trespass, which incurs guilt before God and other human beings. If we say that we have no sin, we deceive ourselves (1 Jn. 8-9). We need God's forgiveness and forgiveness of one another. Remember the parable

41

of the unforgiving servant (Mt. 18:23-35)? Although he was forgiven ten thousand talents, he did not forgive a very small sum in comparison. But when we approach the Benefactor, we should ourselves be benefactors.

Forgive freely being conscious of your likeness to God. Forgive your brothers and sisters in Christ, being reconciled to them, for there is not greater sacrifice to God than peace, concord and unity among the people of God united in the unity of the Father, the Son, and the Holy Spirit. Forgive unbelievers and persecutors, as well, imitating the example of Christ who, "when He was reviled, He did not revile in return; when He suffered, He did not threaten; but He trusted to Him who judges justly" (1 Pt. 2:23; cf. 1 Cor. 4:12; Rm. 12:14-21). Forgive from the heart that you may be free.

"And lead us not into temptation"

What is meant by temptation? There is temptation as inward inclination to evil because of fallen human nature, a soul's own enticement to sin. God has nothing to do with this kind of temptation, for "He tempts no one" (Jm. 1:13-15). There is also temptation, as the Scriptures attest, in the form of many tests, trials, afflictions, and hard labor in life. Indeed all life seems to be a temptation. No one, rich or pour, healthy or sick, famous or unknown, is exempt from hurt and suffering. God does not desire human suffering but permits it because of human freedom. All temptation, whether inward or outward, is ultimately linked to the mystery of free will.

If life is full of temptations, how can we then pray "not to enter" (*me eisenenkeis*) into temptation? Are we not taught to "enter by the narrow gate" (Mt. 7:13), and that no one is saved without temptation and trials? Did not the Apostle Paul himself suffer from a "thorn in the flesh" of which he was not relieved even after fervent prayer (2 Cor. 12:7-10)? We do not therefore pray not to enter into temptation at all but not to be encompassed, overwhelmed, and conquered by temptation, and then abandoned by God in our sins (Rm. 1:24).

It is one thing to be tempted and quite another to fall to sin. Christ said: "Watch and pray that you may not enter into temptation; the spirit indeed is willing, but the flesh is weak" (Mt. 26:41). But even when tempted, God seeks to use temptations positively to give us self-knowledge, awareness of our evils, and spiritual maturity. If you are ready and willing, God "will not let you be tempted beyond your strength, but with the temptation will also provide the way of escape, that you may be able to endure it" (1 Cor. 10:13). Rest assured that "in everything God works for good with those who love Him" (Rm. 8:28) and who cooperate with Him for their salvation.

"But deliver us from evil"

Evil is not abstract evil but personal, the Evil One (*Ho Poneros*). Satan hates humanity and passionately seeks to destroy it by myriad lies, traps and deceptions. He uses temptations for his purposes. But God's power is infinitely stronger. Christ has defeated Satan whom He saw "fall like lightning from heaven" (Lk. 10:18). Under God's protection, we stand secure against the devil and all his works. The devil has no authority over us, unless we willingly submit to him. Nor does he have any power against us, unless God previously permitted it, in order that all our devotion and obedience may be turned to God.

When we pray that we may be delivered from Satan, we pray that he may not prevail against us and defeat us. By God's power we can prevail against him and defeat him. But we need to take to heart St. Paul's counsel: "Be strong in the Lord and in the strength of His might. Put on the whole armor of God, that you may be able to stand against the wiles of the devil" (Eph. 6:10-11). And again: "Be watchful, stand firm in your faith, be courageous, be strong. Let all that you do be done in love" (1 Cor. 16:13).

We have meditated on the Lord's Prayer through the teachings of the Church Fathers. What should my and your response be to the Lord's Prayer? A friend suggested the following applications of the Lord's Prayer by means of a poem entitled "I Cannot Pray:"

I cannot say OUR, if my faith has no room for OTHERS.

I cannot say FATHER, if I do not demonstrate that I am truly His SON or DAUGHTER by grace in my daily living.

I cannot say WHO ART IN HEAVEN, if my interests and pursuits converge on EARTHLY THINGS.

I cannot say HALLOWED BE THY NAME, if my heart and lips are stained with EVIL.

I cannot say THY KINGDOM COME, if I am unwilling to give up my AUTONOMY before the Lordship of God.

I cannot say THY WILL BE DONE, if I seek constantly to fulfill MY OWN WILL.

I cannot say ON EARTH AS IT IS IN
HEAVEN, unless I truly serve Him
HERE AND NOW.

I cannot say GIVE US THIS DAY OUR
DAILY BREAD, without doing HONEST
WORK for it, or by ignoring my
NEIGHBOR'S NEEDS.

I cannot say FORGIVE US OUR TRES-
PASSES AS WE FORGIVE THOSE WHO
TRESPASS AGAINST US, if I continue to
harbor GRUDGES against others.

I cannot say LEAD US NOT INTO TEMP-
TATION, if I choose to remain in a situation where I FALL INTO SIN.

I cannot say DELIVER US FROM EVIL,
if I do not FIGHT AGAINST SIN with
prayer and all my resources.[14]

The Lord's Prayer is concluded with a doxology by
the priest: "For Yours is the kingdom and the power and
the glory of the Father and the Son and the Holy Spirit,
now and forever and to the ages of ages." We praise and
glorify God for His kingdom and power by which He
blesses and protect us. We thank God for the Lord's
Prayer which, so the Church Fathers say, is a summary
of the Gospel and reflects the whole content of Christ's
teaching.

The whole aim and purpose of God, hidden in the
Lord's Prayer, and all true prayer, is the mystery of the
theosis (divinization) of humanity through union with
God. Christ taught us to pray, and to be persistent in
prayer, both by words and deed, for He often prayed
Himself. Prayer was a distinct mark of Jesus' ministry.
Prayer, according to the Church Fathers, is intimacy
with God; the enjoyment of all things present and the
substance of the things to come. A person who does not
unite himself or herself to God through prayer is
separated from God. If work itself is preceded by regular
prayer, sin will find no entrance into the soul because

[14]This piece, which has been slightly modified, was made available
to me by Father Nicholas Triantafilou of Houston, Texas.

the consciousness of God is firmly established in the heart; the devices of the devil remain sterile; and matters of dispute will always be settled according to justice. In a word, prayer is the mystery of sharing the presence, power, and life of God.

Holy Communion

The sun burns brilliantly every day and every hour. It sends an unceasing stream of rays of light and heat to the earth. Although science assures us that one day the sun will burn up, to us the sun now seems unchangeable. Despite the stream of billions of outgoing rays, it remains the same. This is a remarkable phenomenon.

Yet it is only a small analogy by which we can glimpse how Christ, the Sun of Righteousness, comes to us as uncreated and deifying light through Holy Communion. The eternal Christ "is the same yesterday and today and for ever" (Heb. 13:8). As the bread of life He is present whole on all the sacred altars of the Orthodox Churches throughout the ages. As He fed the multitude of men, women, and children in the wilderness by the multiplication of the loaves, He continues to feed multitudes of His people throughout the generations through the eucharistic gifts. When the priest lifts up and breaks the consecrated bread or Lamb, he says: "The Lamb of God is broken and distributed; broken but not divided. He is for ever eaten yet is never consumed, but He sanctifies those who partake of Him."[15]

Proschomen! Let us be attentive! The holy gifts for the holy people of God! These are the calls to attention which, as we already know but saw again in our video program, bring us to the awesome moment of Holy Communion. In an earlier mystical prayer the priest invokes Christ to come in our midst and Himself give Holy Communion first to the priest by His own mighty hand and then to all the people through the priest.

The celebrant lifts up and breaks the Lamb, placing three particles back on the paten and one particle in the chalice, saying: "The fulness of the Holy Spirit." After blessing the hot water (*zeon*), a symbol of divine life, he pours hot water into the cup with the consecrated wine,

[15]The above images and thoughts are taken from Kantiotes, *On the Divine Liturgy*, Vol. 2, p. 255.

46

saying: "The warmth of the Holy Spirit" (or according to a more recent version, "The warmth of faith, filled with the Holy Spirit"). The priest recites the communion prayers and himself receives Holy Communion. He prepares to commune the people by placing the three remaining particles of the Lamb from the paten into the cup. He then lifts up the cup, turns to the congregation, and offers Holy Communion in the greatest act of invitation ever possible, calling to the people: "Approach with the fear of God, faith, and love!"

With what feelings and thoughts should we approach Holy Communion? What is the meaning of Holy Communion for you? How often do you receive Holy Communion? Why? Or, why not? What impact does Holy Communion have upon your inner being? What consequences do you draw from Holy Communion for daily living? St. John Chrysostom writes:

> Consider with what an honor you have been honored, of what table you are partaking. The One before whom the angels tremble, when they behold Him, and dare not look up without awe because of the brightness which comes from Him— by Him are we fed, with Him we are commingled, and we are made the one body and one flesh of Christ. "Who

shall declare the mighty works of the Lord? Who shall cause all His praises to be heard" (Ps. 105:2)?[16]

By partaking of Holy Communion we respond to the greatest invitation and receive the highest honor. The Liturgy itself tells us with what feelings and thoughts we should approach Holy Communion. "Approach with the fear of God, faith, and love?!"

But why fear of God? Because Holy Communion is divine fire. When the prophet Isaiah was overwhelmed by his sense of sinfulness before the vision of the glory of God, an angel of the Lord touched his lips with a burning coal in an act of cleansing and said to him: "Behold, this has touched your lips; your guilt is taken away, and your sin forgiven" (Is. 6:7), words which the priest repeats after he has received Holy Communion.

Holy Communion is like live coal. Burning coal is not just coal, but coal penetrated with fire. The eucharistic gifts are not merely bread and wine, but bread and wine glowing with the fire of Christ's divinity, His uncreated grace. One of the communion prayers says: "Behold, I approach for Holy Communion. O Creator, sear me not as I partake— for You are fire which burns the unworthy— but cleanse me from every stain." Another communion prayer states: "Burn away with Your immaterial fire my sins and make me worthy to be filled with your joy." In the words of St. John of Damascus:

> Let us approach it (Holy Commun-
> ion) with burning desire...Let us par-
> take of the Divine Coal, in order that the
> fire of the longing in us, with the addi-
> tional heat received from the Coal, may
> completely burn up our sins and illu-
> mine our hearts, and that we may be
> inflamed and divinized by association
> with the divine fire.[17]

---

[16]*Homily on Matthew*, 82. 5, cited by Sheerin, *The Eucharist*, p. 290.

[17]*Exposition of the Orthodox Faith*, 86, cited by Sheerin, p. 171.

We approach Holy Communion also with faith. Who is worthy of this heavenly gift? Who is sufficiently holy to be united with divine fire? We sing: "One is holy, One is Lord, Jesus Christ, to the glory of God the Father!1" Out of reverence for the sacrament there has developed over many centuries a tradition of receiving Holy Communion only three or four times a year. But the great Church Fathers teach us that we are to partake of it frequently, if possible even daily (St. Basil).[18]

Holy Communion is offered in order to be received. The Eucharist is complete with the partaking of Holy Communion, not without it. Who would be invited and go to dinner at a friend's home and insult the host by not eating? How can we as invited guests reject the invitation of eating at His table by Christ the King? It is an awesome act of which no one is worthy, yet divinely commanded: "Take, eat...Drink of it all of you!" St. John Chrysostom observes that "to approach carelessly is perilous" but "not to share in these mystical suppers is (spiritual) famine and death."[19] Again St. John asks: "Are you prepared? Receive Holy Communion every day. Are you not prepared? Then don't receive it even on Easter!"[20]

So it is that we approach with faith, as conscious of the heavenly gift as we are conscious of our unworthiness. Being prepared means, as Father Calivas says in the video, coming to Holy Communion in a state of repentance, forgiving one another, being reconciled to one another, being loving human beings, and striving to fulfil God's commandments in daily life. We also prepare by appropriate fasting. A special preparation, as well, is praying without fail the communion prayers on the previous evening, the morning, and during the Eucharist. Despite all these preparations, when the moment comes, we still approach Holy Communion with faith as the woman with the issue of blood who humbly touched Jesus and was instantly healed (Mt. 9:20-22). We come believing that the Lord, as a communion hymn confesses, is "truly the Son of the living God, who came into the world to save sinners, of whom I am the first;" and believing that Holy Communion is

[18]See Sheerin, pp. 304-305.
[19]Homily on First Corinthians, 24.5, cited by Sheerin, p. 296.
[20]Quoted by Kantiotes, Vol. 2, p. 269.

truly His pure body and precious blood. We come as the convicted thief on the cross, asking for Christ's mercy and saying: "Jesus, remember me when you come into Your kingdom" (Lk. 23:42).

We approach Holy Communion, as well, with love. "Greater love has no one than this," said Jesus, "that one should lay down one's life for one's friends" (Jn 16:13). By an excess of love Christ died for us and now offers Himself to us through the eucharistic gifts. Earlier in the Eucharist, when the priest calls to the worshipers, "Let us love one another," the priest offers a brief mystical prayer from the Psalms: "I love You, O Lord, my strenghth. The Lord is my rock, and my fortress, and my deliverer" (Ps. 18:1). With the love and assurance of this verse from the Psalms should we all go forward to partake of Holy Communion. In the words of a communion hymn: "It is good for me to cling to God and to place in Him the hope of my salvation." Holy Communion is a divine clinging, an intimate union of love in which the heart absorbs the Lord and the Lord absorbs the heart. We can say with St. Paul: "It is no longer I who live, but Christ who lives in me" (Gal. 2:20). We should be as eager to be united with the King of love and be fed by His divine love, so teach the Church Fathers and saints, as an infant is eager to be united with its mother and be fed by her milk.

Through Holy Communion we participate at the table of love. We eat of the bread of love. We become ourselves love, for our hearts are filled with love. Divine love is the greatest power in the universe. By partaking of it we are changed from small selfish creatures to kings of creation in the likeness of Christ. What can be more powerful and transforming than the love of Him who sits on the right hand of the glory of the Father and yet humbly offers Himself as food in Holy Communion? To quote again a striking passage from St. John Chrysostom:

> Christ has done this very thing to urge us on to greater love; and to show the love He has for us, He has made it possible for those who desire, not merely to look upon Him, but even to touch Him and to eat Him and to fix their teeth in His flesh, and to be commingled with Him, and to satisfy all their long-

ing. Let us, then, come back from that table like lions breathing fire, thus becoming terrifying to the devil, and remaining mindful of our Head (Christ) and of the love which He has shown for us.[21]

Indeed, like lions breathing spiritual fire! Whatever failings and weaknesses we may have, however sinful we may be, the act of Holy Communion when approached with "fear of God, faith, and love," is an act of joy, praise, and thanksgiving; an experience of the triumph of grace over sin and of life over death. "Save, O God, Your people and bless Your inheritance," cries out the priest as he raises high the sacred gifts after Holy Communion. The worshipers then triumphantly resound: "We have seen the true light; we have received the heavenly Spirit; we have found the true faith, worshiping the undivided Trinity; for the Trinity has saved us!"

The Dismissal

A story is told about a lady who was rushing to Church late and arrived just as the priest was closing the front doors. She ran up to him gasping: "Are services over?" "No, madam," the priest replied weighing his words: "Worship is over. The services are just beginning."

The dismissal, which is the last part of the Liturgy, tells us that the Liturgy is ending but it also tells us that services are just beginning. An integral part of the Liturgy from ancient times, the dismissal is far from being just a ceremonial conclusion. The "amen," too, which we say at the end of prayers, is not a mechanical sign saying "This is the end". The "amen" means: "So be it!" It is a profound affirmation of what has been said and done. It expresses the full agreement of the worshiper with the requests, truths, and blessings of the prayers and liturgical acts. It is a seal of commitment, a signature carrying important promises. So also the dismissal is a profound affirmation of the total meaning of the Liturgy, its blessings and challenges, carrying important consequences for daily living.

"Let us depart in peace!" the priest calls out to the people. This is the keynote of the dismissal. A better

---

[21]*Homily on the Gospel of John*, 46, cited by Sheerin, p. 205.

translation of the very *proelthomen* is "go forth." The worshipers are not asked simply to depart, that is, to leave or go away, but precisely to go forth, that is, to go forward into the world as active witnesses of Christ. Father Schmemann has commented that in the Liturgy we have ascended Mount Tabor, the mount of transfiguration; in the dismissal we are sent back into the world to be heralds of the gifts that we have received, the "true Light," the "heavenly Spirit," and the "true faith." The Eucharist was the end of the journey into the kingdom; and now the dismissal is a beginning in the task of ordinary living. But there is a difference. Through the Liturgy God has empowered us and "has made us *competent*— competent to be His witnesses, to fulfil what He has done and is ever doing." This is the essential connection between the Liturgy and our life in the world. "The mission of the Church begins in the liturgy of ascension...(which) makes possible the liturgy of mission."[22]

How are we to go out into the world? What are your thoughts when the priest says: "Let us go forth?" With what dispositions do you go out into the world? What connections do you draw between your experience of the Liturgy and your ordinary life? With what equipment are you spiritually equipped to face the challenges, duties, and problems of daily living? What does it mean to you to receive the *antidoron* or blessed bread from the priest's hand and then walk out of Church into the world?

The concluding part of the Liturgy, which includes the dismissal, helps us to find several important answers to these questions. After having celebrated the Eucharist and received Holy Communion, we are to go out into the world above all with thankful and joyful hearts. An ancient thanksgiving hymn chanted after Holy Communion, when the priest takes the eucharistic gifts from the Holy Table to the Prothesis, resounds with these words: "Let our mouths be filled with Your praise, Lord, that we may sing of Your glory...Alleluia, alleluia, alleluia!" In a mystical prayer at the Prothesis the priest prays: "Christ our God,....fill our hearts with joy and gladness!" The last hymn of the Liturgy, repeated three times, is a thankful doxology: "Blessed is

[22]Alexander Schmemann, *For the Life of the World*, pp. 45-46.

the name of the Lord, both now and to the ages!" It is not without special meaning that this thankful doxology was first uttered by the much afflicted Job (Job 1:21). "The example Job give us is that, no matter what our situation might be, and no matter how many sorrows and temptations we encounter, we should always give words of thanks to God."[23] The Liturgy is our assurance that Christ is with us to the end of time. Through the Liturgy we hear His voice again in our hearts, saying: "Be of good cheer, I have overcome the world" (Jn 16:33). Christ's victory and His presence in us enable us to go forth in the world with thankful and joyful hearts. Blessed be the name of the Lord forever!

The keynote of the dismissal sends out the worshipers with the gift of peace: "Go forth in peace!" We pray for peace many times during the Liturgy. The priest also blesses the congregation several times with the blessing of peace: "Peace be with you." How much we need true peace in our lives! Peace in our emotions. Peace in our thoughts. Peace in our personal affairs. Peace in our families. Peace in the world.

Through the Liturgy we meet the Prince of Peace who offered His life on the Cross, God's great act of reconciliation with humanity, the ground and source of all peace. Before one can enjoy the peace of God, however, he or she must first be reconciled to God, that is, have peace with God. The Liturgy as a sacrifice is a continuous act of reconciliation in which we find forgiveness and renewal through union with Christ who died and rose in order to give us true and abiding peace. "Peace I leave with you," Christ said; "my peace I give to you; not as the world gives do I give to you" (Jn 14:27). The Christ whom we receive in the Eucharist and who lives in our hearts, is both our peace with God and our peace of God. Insofar as we put ourselves into the Liturgy and receive Christ's peace as a gift of the Holy Spirit, we can go out into the world with peace and also as peacemakers— heralds and agents of peace.

A highlight of the dismissal is the blessing of the congregation as a concluding liturgical act. Just before the prayer of dismissal (apolysis) the priest turns to the congregation, makes the sign of the cross over them,

---

[23]Kantiotes, On the Liturgy, Vol. 2, p. 279.

and pronounces this blessing: "May the blessing of the Lord and His mercy come upon you through His divine grace and love always!" In the previous public prayer offered before the icon of Christ or in front of the congregation, the priest prays: "Lord, bless those who praise You and sanctify those who trust in You." We are to go out into the world blessed and sanctified by God. We know that Christ, whom we have received in the Eucharist, is our sanctification, just as the priest earlier has said: "You are our sanctification and to You we give glory." Sanctification is a gift but also a purpose, *the* purpose, for living. Listen to these words of Bishop Augoustinos:

> Most people live for other purposes. Some live for riches; others, for pleasures and amusements; some for fame and glory; and still others for knowledge. There is no thought of sanctification or eternal life. Others, however, believe in Christ and listen to His divine teaching, for they know that beyond any worldly purpose, there is a divine purpose for living, that is, to become holy. "Be holy; for I am holy" (Lev. 20:7; 1 Pt. 1:16).[24]

[24]*Ibid,* p. 275.

We have concluded our study of the Divine Liturgy. As the video program pointed out at the end, the Divine Liturgy shows us life as it ought to be lived; it manifests the true dimensions of the Christian life. The Liturgy manifests the Church; it shows what the Church is and ought to be as brothers and sisters united in Christ, the mystical body of Christ, transcending all prejudices and barriers, possessing a strong sense of community, and renewing itself over against the corroding influences of society. But the Church continues to be the Church after the Liturgy, a loving community called to live the new and higher quality of life which is neither expected nor to be found in society. There is, as we noted, a liturgy after the Liturgy; a liturgy of life in which Christians ought to maintain strong relationships, be involved in the lives of one another, and serve as the eyes, hands, and feet of Christ wherever God has place them.

In the Liturgy you receive Holy Communion which is, to use an image of Chrysostom, like molten gold. Let your mouth, your heart, your thoughts, your whole being and life, be golden for the glory of Christ. You take the *antidoron*, kissing the priest's hand, and going out into the world. Let this be a symbol of the gift of Christ, whom you receive in the Liturgy and are called to share with others in the world. As Father Calivas stated in the closing shot of the video, each Liturgy is new, a new encounter with Christ, renewing your life so that it can impact upon society: "One life touched by God can make a difference." The prayers of the Theotokos, the angels, and of all the saints accompany our life's journey. May the joy of the Divine Liturgy always be with all of us so that your life and mine, transformed by God can make a difference.

4

RENEWAL THROUGH THE LITURGY

What is Renewal?

We have talked about the Divine Liturgy as a jewel, a precious gift which the Church has received from the hands of Christ Himself. Through the Liturgy Christ comes to us and lives in us. Through the Liturgy we have our being "in Christ," growing and being recreated according to the image and likeness of Christ. St. Paul has written: "If any one is in Christ, he (or she) is a new creation (or new creature); the old has passed away, behold, the new has come" (2 Cor. 5:17).

But what is the new that has come? What is a new creation or new creature? What do we mean when we talk about renewal? Renewal can mean many things to many people. The dictionary says that "to renew" means "to make like new," "refresh," "rejuvenate," "restore to freshness, vigor or perfection." Renewal is "the act or process of renewing" and also "the quality or state of being renewed." In this book by renewal we mean Orthodox spiritual renewal, Orthodox spirituality, or Orthodox life, rooted in the Bible and interpreted by the Church Fathers.

Christ, as someone has said, did not come to make speeches but to make disciples. He did not come to create a theological system but a living organism, the Church. In the same spirit the Church Fathers have taught us that Orthodox spirituality has less to do with abstract talk and much more to do with Christian living. True spirituality is not what is described ideally by books but what emanates from actual persons. Thus, Orthodox spirituality or Orthodox renewal is ordinary Orthodox Christian life lived in depth, sensitivity, and fullness: life centered on Christ and the fruit of the Spirit—faith, joy, peace, and love; life based on the sacraments of the Church and ongoing personal prayer; life meant for daily living, family relationships, friendships, human interactions, work, and play; life touched by a paschal radiance even in the face of pain and suffering.

The 28th Biennial Clergy-Laity Congress of the Greek Orthodox Archdiocese in Dallas, Texas (1986) had as its theme to "grow in grace and in the knowledge of our Lord and Savior Jesus Christ" (2 Pt. 3:18). In the keynote address to the Congress, His Eminence Archbishop Iakovos spoke powerfully on the topic of "Rekindling an Orthodox Awareness." After many generations of growth in membership, church buildings, and various institutions, Archbishop Iakovos pointed out, "it is of utmost importance now to concentrate on a basic and very fundamental growth in the grace and knowledge of our Lord and Savior Jesus Christ."[1] The Archbishop challenged clergy and laity alike to become more conscious members of the body of Christ, to let their Orthodox consciousness be enflamed by the faith that we have been saved by grace and that God has already raised us up and has made us sit together in the heavenly places in Christ (Eph. 2:5-6). His Eminence also added that young men and women expect their parishes to be spiritually vibrant, concerned with moral and spiritual matters, laboring to enhance the quality of people's lives, building up character, teaching the Orthodox Faith, and inviting the communicants to the mystical Supper of Christ. He then applied these reflections on all aspects of the Archdiocese including the clergy, laity, parish, diocese, seminary, and youth.

There is no doubt that we need a rekindling of our Orthodox consciousness today. We need Orthodox renewal not only because of the moral dangers and vain trivialities of modern society, but also because newness is always intrinsic to Christian life. Many seem to have forgotten, or neglect, or simply pay lip service to spiritual life and the spiritual world. Yet people are starving for spiritual food, a sense of communion with the divine, an experience of transcendence beyond what is tangible, and thus seek to satisfy this need even in warped, dehumanizing, and demonic ways such as through drugs, bizzare films, wild music, and the occult.

In the face of this hunger, as well as these distortions, we cannot allow Orthodoxy to be understood and lived simply as administration of church affairs, sociocultural activities, and ceremonial formalism. We must not permit the inner glow of Orthodox spiritual life to lie hidden underneath ashes in a fancy fireplace. Consider that the average Orthodox person may well take Christian faith and Church almost completely for granted, more or less as a marginal formality, having little to do with daily decisions about business, recreation, friend-

[1]Archbishop Iakovos, "Rekindling an Orthodox Awareness," Keynote Address to the 28th Biennial Clergy-Laity Congress, June 29, 1986, Dallas, Texas, published by the Greek Orthodox Archdiocese of North and South America, p. 1.

ships, moral challenges, and political life. Consider also that an Orthodox person can grow up nearly at the center of the life of the Church, sing in the choir, participate in youth programs, even become a lay or ordained leader and, paradoxically, not seem to be really convinced that the Church can truly live by the spirit of Christ and can truly accomplish the essentials goals commissioned to it by Christ.

At the heart of the challenge of Orthodox spiritual renewal is the shifting of the Orthodox mindset from a formal mode to a more personal mode within the framework of Orthodox doctrine. The Orthodox Church in its outward life has been for many centuries becoming increasingly formalistic, cultic, and even legalistic. For example, the Liturgy itself to many is a formal sacred ceremony quite separated from ordinary profane life.

But true worship according to Christ is not an outwardly pious or cultic act but a way of life. Christ has inaugurated a new life, not a new "religion" or new cult, that is to say, a human religious system by which to try to reach God. Indeed Christian worship in general and the Eucharist in particular, writes Alexander Schmemann, are the end of cult, of the sacred religious act isolated from the profane life of the community.[2] Admittedly formalism has been a factor of endurance and perpetuity in history. But in the modern, pluralistic, changing, and open world a formalistic Church experiences an identity crisis because the formal faith and loyalty of its adherents can no longer be taken for granted.

The answer to this situation is a more personal approach to the Orthodox faith and life. By personal I mean an internalization of the faith, worship, and truths of Orthodoxy so that we actually do what we proclaim and we actually show ourselves to be what we say we are. Internalization is a deep penetration of the consciousness by Orthodox values, a dynamic inner transformation in the context of personal integrity, humility, and love, reflecting the spirit of Christ, especially on the part of lay and ordained leaders of the Church who are the examples and potential bearers of a true Orthodox spiritual renewal.

[2]See Schmemann, *For the Life of the World*, pp. 20 and 25-26.

What is a fact is that we can no longer count on the investments of the past, that is, on the power of tradition and formal habits. We must generate new spiritual investments ourselves in a changing and open society just as the Apostles and great Church Fathers did in their own times. The rekindling of an Orthodox awareness worthy of its name cannot be envisioned apart from such a personal approach to Orthodox faith and life which alone can inwardly energize the Orthodox people and eventually make the Church credible even to avowed opponents of the Christian way of life in our own days.

If we desire it, there are many ways through which by God's grace we can pursue Orthodox renewal. One way is concentration on the meaning and preaching of the gospel which offers the gift of salvation, invites to repentance, and calls for a life of commitment. The gospel as a divine message has the power to generate faith, motivation, and enthusiasm to come to Christ, to accept Christ as Savior and God, and to do all things for Christ. Another way is to rejuvenate participation in worship, one of the most powerful transforming forces in the life of the Church. A fervent faith needs fervent worship for expression and inspiration toward action. Practical matters such as teaching people how to worship, explaining the meaning of liturgical acts, hymns, and prayers, and finding specific ways to involve them actively in worship, are crucial.

We need to do the same with private prayer and personal devotions. The impression is that Orthodox Christians are not praying much, and if they are, it is in a quick, perfunctory way. Even we clergy are deficient in regular prayer, scriptural reading and meditation, and reading of the saints. Yet what is more important to nourishing personal spirituality, maintaining a warm personal relationship with the risen Christ, and consequently with our fellow human beings, than these devotions? Still there are other ways of rekindling the Orthodox awareness through effective Christian education, youth programs, service projects, and mission.

Why does the Divine Liturgy deserve special attention in the call for Orthodox renewal? It does so for both practical and theological reasons. On the practical level the Liturgy is the main and most frequent gathering of all the people, young and old, men and women, married and single, active and less active. A youth program will attract a number of the youth. A retreat will draw those who have cultivated spiritual interests. Other special programs will help those with special needs and interests. But the Liturgy is for all and at the center of our worship. Sunday after Sunday the Liturgy is the regular meeting of the community. An effective and participatory Liturgy can concretely impact at once on the whole community toward Orthodox renewal. On a theological and spiritual level the Divine Liturgy is the highest moment of our experience of and communion with Christ. When we come to understand the Liturgy as a corporate fervent prayer of praise and thanksgiving, then we can also appreciate that in the Liturgy , as Nicholas Cabasilas writes: "Christ Himself is present (and) implants the very essence of life into our souls in an ineffable manner."[3] Through the Liturgy Christ recreates and renews us continuously. He is the One who descends from His throne of glory and says: "Behold, I make all things new" (Rev. 21:5).

Attitudes to the Liturgy

In one of his discourses St. Symeon the New Theologian describes himself as a *ptochos philadelphos*— a poor beggar who loves his fellow beggars. Just as such a loving beggar, when finding a kind and merciful Christian who gave him a coin joyfully tells his fellow beggars to go get some, too, so also St. Symeon having received God's love and mercy earnestly calls to his fellow human beings to do the same. Run, brothers and sisters, run! I cannot endure to enjoy the gift alone; I cannot hide it in my pocket. I lay it bare on the palm of my hand. And the Giver is such that He will not be angry but will be pleased that I told you about Him and His wealth![4]

Although St. Symeon discovered the love and mercy of God through deep personal prayer and repentance, we can apply his illustration to the Liturgy. We are all humble beggars who share through the Liturgy in the inexhaustible wealth of God who delights in giving it away. Faithful and informed Orthodox Christians recognize the value of the Divine Liturgy as the gift of

[3]*The Life in Christ*, p. 49.
[4]Symeon the New Theologian, *The Discourses*, trans. C. J. deCatanzaro (Paulist Pres, 1980), pp. 348-349.

Christ. They show it by their attitude to the Liturgy. They leave their homes on time in order to be present for the beginning of the Liturgy and to hear the priest's solemn doxological invocation: "Blessed is the kingdom

of the Father and the Son and the Holy Spirit." They try to arrive in a prayerful spirit or at least ready to collect their thoughts for sincere prayer. They try to put their whole selves into the Liturgy. Although they are not always completely successful, they experience a closeness with God, a sense of His loving forgiveness and cleansing, a renewal of personal faith and life in Christ. Having found the Liturgy a source of healing and strength, they leave the Church as renewed people ready to meet the challenges of daily living with the joyous presence of the Holy Spirit. They are also inwardly eager, if not always outwardly ready, to share the wondrous miracle of the Liturgy with others: Run, friend, run! Discover for yourself the refreshing fountain of living water ! For such Christians Sunday is not the last day of the week, but truly the first, the Lord's Day, the day on which they receive the gift of Christ, which is more valuable than all the treasures of the earth.

However, these faithful and informed Orthodox Christians make up not the majority, but only the minority of baptized Orthodox. The majority views the Liturgy in other ways. The rules of conduct seem to be lateness, passivity, irregularity, infrequent Holy Communion, absence from evening or weekday services, and general boredom with prayer and worship. Why?

Some view the Liturgy as a religious obligation. They may fulfil it as a matter of habit. In other cases they may fulfil it earnestly— at least try to do so— in order somehow to be on the good side of God. Many others think of the Liturgy basically as a religious ceremony, a kind of sacred liturgical production by the priest, choir and/or chanter. They, too, may attend out of habit. In other cases they may attend when convenient, more or less as spectators. Any one from this category can experience a sense of religious awe from time to time and most want also to keep in touch with the people of the parish. Still others hardly think of the Divine Liturgy at all. They seem totally preoccupied with their own private, family, business, and social affairs. Nevertheless they may attend Church on Christmas and Easter. They may even make an occasional monetary contribution to the Church to help out the community.

Such are the various attitudes with which most Orthodox unfortunately seem to approach the Liturgy. These Christians may also share a number of things in common. They usually come late and want services to be over as soon as possible. While their bodies are in Church, their minds most of the time are not. They find the Liturgy extremely tiring. They get little or nothing out of it. Efforts by the priest to have them participate actively are bothersome and distracting to their own world of thought. What is worse, they may leave the Church much as they came, unchanged by the wondrous mystery of the Eucharist and apparently unaware of any significant consequences of the Liturgy for daily living.

There are shades and degrees of positions between all of the above categories of Orthodox Christians and their various attitudes to the Divine Liturgy. Too, it cannot be said that Orthodox Christians who are neglectful of the spiritual treasure of the Liturgy are necessarily lacking in devotion to the Church. Quite the contrary, some may be among the strongest members of the local Church as they understand it. They may have an implicit faith which needs to be cultivated and be made explicit.

However, the overall picture of the effectiveness of the Liturgy in the actual life of baptized Orthodox Christians, speaking honestly, presents a tragedy. The jewel in the jewel box seems forgotten or ignored. The priceless gift of Christ is not recognized for its supreme worth. It is even superficially treated. The people of God seem to have become unmindful of Jesus' warning about how to keep what is holy and how to treat the pearls of faith (Mt. 7:6). The results are calamitous spiritually. Many bear the name of Orthodox Christian but not the substance of it. They follow the formal rites of the Church but are not transformed by them. The lack of spiritual vitality, not to say even of spiritual orientation, in the daily life of many Orthodox Christians, gives sad evidence of the fact that the Divine Liturgy is not, what it is meant to be.

A Spiritual Re-awakening

But it was not always so. Nor should it by any means remain so. We must not continue in complacent attitudes and sinful habits simply because we may be conditioned by them. To do so in the present days of moral confusion and spiritual agony is to compound the tragedy. Rather we must re-awaken to the gift of Christ offered through the Liturgy, receive it in our hearts, and allow it to energize our whole beings, just as the Church Fathers, Saints and early Christians did. To quote Bishop Augoustinos again:

> In the early days of the Church, the Christians, moved by faith, would attend the Liturgy with deep feeling, their eyes filled with tears and their hearts with true prayers. Let us pray that we may see the return of those days.[5]

How can a re-awakening of this magnitude take place? All of the people of God, with the guidance of their leaders, must approach this challenge with faith, prayer, love, commitment, and reliance on the grace of God. We need not begin with a lot of fanfare. But we do need to begin with true repentance, a conversion of the heart to Christ dwelling in us. Results cannot be expected overnight. But what must be expected are patient, prayerful labor, and faithful, consistent pursuit of the essential task. What is the essential task?

[5]*On the Divine Liturgy*, Vol. I, p. 14.

Nothing less than a steady focus on Church priorities, policies, and activities in the perspective of the Divine Liturgy. Granted, of course, the celebration of the Liturgy is not the only ministry of the Church. There are other important ministries—evangelism, mission, education, pastoral care, and philanthropy. But the Liturgy is the highest expression of our experience of Christ and the focus of the life of the Church. A spiritual re-awakening centered on the Liturgy impacts on all of us personally and corporately. Such a spiritual re-awakening, as well, enlivens and integrates all the ministries of the Church.

Do talks, conferences, seminars, and retreats help? These are helpful and should continue. Yet these attract persons who already have clear spiritual interests and influence a limited number of people. The rank-and-file Orthodox Christian must also be challenged at more practical levels of Church life in which he or she is likely to be involved: the parish council, the philoptochos society, the choir, the youth group, and so on. What does the role of the parish council and its work have to do with the Divine Liturgy? What is the purpose of the philoptochos in the light of the Liturgy? How does the choir best fulfil its purpose in the Liturgy? How does a youth group function if the Liturgy is taken seriously? How do a family, married couple, single person, student, teacher, office worker, business person, live and conduct themselves, when life and thought are anchored on the Liturgy?

These and similar questions can be raised with profit by all because every baptized Orthodox Christian is a bearer of the Spirit and therefore an agent of truth. And such questions deserve applied as well as abstract answers. The cutting edge of a true spiritual re-awakening is a sincere willingness to put into practice at every step of the way whatever insights or truths are discovered by asking these kinds of questions. We need to help one another live out the truths of the Orthodox Faith in concrete terms in the actual context of the life of the Church. The challenge of each Orthodox Christian lay or ordained, is to ponder directly what is my own experience of Christ, my own participation in the Liturgy, my own conduct in the light of the Liturgy, and to take appropriate action.

In this perspective the whole character and mission of the Church as a living Church become powerfully clear. The Liturgy can even be applied to the administrative structures of the Church. Approached in the spirit of the Liturgy, the nature, goals, and methodology of local parish assemblies take on spiritual content, although dealing with ordinary agenda items, and also reinforce spiritual growth. Diocese assemblies, too, can be more effective and more edifying when centered on the meaning and celebration of the Liturgy. Even the Biennial Clergy-Laity Congress of our Archdiocese can be organized and conducted so that all aspects of the life of the Church, from setting the budget to facing urgent social issues, can be considered and resolved in the light of the celebration and theology of the Liturgy. What a joyous renewal by God's grace can in this way be experienced by large segments of God's people not in some isolated retreat center but in the very ordinary and concrete life of the Church!

Three Urgent Goals

To pursue the main goal of re-awakening to the value of the gift of Christ offered through the Liturgy, there are three urgent, intermediate goals: (a) re-kindling personal faith, (b) learning about the Liturgy, and (c) participating actively in the Liturgy. These goals are mutually supportive. For example, personal faith motivates a person to learn about the Liturgy and learning about the Liturgy helps one to participate actively in it. But participating actively in the Liturgy, too, can create interest in learning about the Liturgy, and both can activate faith. While these goals reinforce one another because they are closely connected, it is also important to reflect on them separately.

Strive sincerely for a re-kindling of personal faith. By faith we mean not a vague kind of trust that things will get better, for it sometimes happens that they get worse, but specific trust in the Triune God, Father, Son, and Holy Spirit, a personal God who lives and acts in our lives. Personal faith is a conscious commitment and deep desire to live under the lordship of God who has revealed Himself through definite acts, truths, commandments, and purposes, all of which are immensely important to His specific plan for each one of us.

The God of Scripture is personal and each human being is personal, created in His image and likeness.

True faith can, therefore, be only personal, a spiritual bond of trust which is lived deep in the heart as an ongoing personal relationship, much as in the case of a marriage or a friendship. Only personal faith is truly a living, active faith, a faith which brings inner thoughts, motivations, feelings, strengths, weaknesses, choices, and actions before the presence of the living Christ making everything captive to Christ.

What is then meant by re-kindling? Those who have watched fireplaces know that they burn at various levels of intensity. Some have roaring fires. Others burn with medium strength. Others smoulder and give off a lot of smoke. Still others seem to contain only ashes but, when stirred, show glowing embers which can start a new fire. Faith receives its burning energy from the grace of the Holy Spirit. But to act, the Holy Spirit requires open minds and receptive hearts. He will not light his fire in us against our will. Re-kindling personal faith essentially means helping people to come to a conscious decision about the living God and supporting them to live out that decision so that the Holy Spirit can act in their lives. Re-kindling occurs in a heart which has made a conscious choice of a way of life based on Christ and Orthodox spirituality as distinct from various secular ways of living.

The re-kindling of personal faith is neither an isolated event, nor the Spirit working through a single approach. Personal faith is born, activated, and enlivened in a dynamic process of many events and various ways in a given Christian community. Preaching the good news of Christ in the Spirit gives birth to new faith. The example of love and the new quality of life visible in Church members reinforce faith. A disciplined life of prayer and devotional reading energize faith. Clear teaching enriches faith. Effective pastoral care supports faith. Worship, service, and mission give expression to and also strengthen faith. The Spirit works through all these ways in willing persons to re-kindle personal faith. He ignites again and again the fire of living faith which grows brighter and brighter. The whole saving work of the Church converges on this miracle of generating, nurturing, and witnessing to living faith as the pulsating heartbeat of the Church. Only in the context of deep prayerful concern for and action toward the re-kindling of personal faith can we talk about a true re-awakening to the gift of Christ through the Liturgy.

Learning about the Liturgy. The Greek word *mathetes* (disciple) means "learner". A Christian is a learner; a learner of the Word of God, a learner of the ways of God, a learner of the worship of God. To learn something well means to appreciate more deeply its meaning and to be able to accomplish it more effectively. Without being a learner one cannot become a practitioner.

In the case of the Liturgy it is not necessary that one become a liturgiologist, an expert in the historical origins and complex development of the Liturgy in Christian tradition, but a basic understanding of the Liturgy is required for meaningful participation in its celebration. Why do we celebrate the Liturgy? What is the essential meaning of the Liturgy? What are the major parts of the Liturgy and how do they relate to one another? What are some of the symbolic acts and these of the Liturgy? How should the Orthodox Christian participate in the Liturgy? What results and consequences should he or she expect from the celebration of the Liturgy? How is the Liturgy connected to life? Knowing the answers to these questions deepens one's understanding of the Liturgy and prepares one for a fuller participation in its celebration. The intended purpose of this small book is to help people achieve this objective.

Participating actively in the Liturgy. Knowing about and participating in the Liturgy are not identical. One can have an expert knowledge of the Liturgy but not truly participate actively in its mystery. Of course one can also participate deeply in the Liturgy without having a profound knowledge of the Liturgy. All this is to say that participating actively in the Liturgy is a very special factor in its own right, a factor of considerable magnitude for the miracle of the birth of living faith and for the re-awakening to the gift of Christ through the Liturgy. Father Stanley Harakas, Archbishop Iakovos Professor of Orthodox Theology at Holy Cross Greek Orthodox School of Theology, deserves the credit for writing on the importance of active participation in the Liturgy and for providing invaluable practical guidance in achieving it. He has done so in his book *Living the*

Liturgy[6] and in a brief essay *The Melody of Prayer: How to Personally Experience The Divine Liturgy*[7] summarizing the book. Both are highly recommended for personal and group use.

Father Harakas has a decisive answer to the recurrent complaint "I Don't Get Anything Out of Going to Church." Behind this complaint, he says, lies the fact that the majority of Orthodox Christians, young and old, "in their most honest moments, express an inward dissatisfaction with attendance at the Divine Liturgy." It is true that very often, he goes on to say, "sincere Orthodox Christians, willing and eager to find the worship of their Church meaningful and inspiring, [are] disappointed." Many have tried to respond to this serious pastoral problem by placing the responsibility on the celebration of the Liturgy itself, that is, the language of the service, the length of the Liturgy, its relevance for people's lives today, the abilities of the priest, chanter, and choir.

Without denying the relative importance of these factors, Father Harakas decisively shifts the focus of the responsibility to the Christian worshiper himself or herself! The primary answer to the "deplorable situation" regarding the Liturgy is each worshiper's personal responsibility translated into active participation— this is the heart of the matter!

Let not the worshiper wait until the voices of the singers improve. He or she must work, yes work, in

[6]Light and Life Publishing Company (1974).
[7]Light and Life Publishing Company (1979).

order to succeed in the experience of worship, just as he or she must work to get an education, or to maintain a home, or to keep a job, or to live as a Christian in the world. The passive attitude of sitting back on the pew and waiting to be inspired (entertained?) by the other "performers" of the Liturgy must once for all cease. The worshiper himself or herself is and always must be a "performer" in the worship of the Church. The word "Liturgy" means "the work of the people!" The worshiper must come to Church asking "What is my work in the Liturgy?" and be prepared actively to do his or her part in the work of the worship of God. To quote Father Harakas:

> You must give in order to receive. If you really expect to "get something" out of Church attendance, you must give. It is not enough just to sit in Church. You must take an active part in its worship. You must learn to participate personally and individually in the Service. This takes some effort...Active participation ...is the key to successful and meaningful attendance at the Divine Liturgy.[8]

Once this foundation stone is in place, namely, the personal responsibility of the Christian in worship, a second issue arises. How is the mystical and ceremonial grandeur of the Liturgy to be bridged with the consciousness of the worshiper sitting in the pew who is willing actively to participate in the Liturgy? In other words, granted that the worshiper comes to Church ready to share in the work of the worship of God, what is his or her work, and how is one to do it? The usual advice to "observe" and "follow along" during the Liturgy is not a sufficient answer. Father Harakas discovered that the very drama of the ritual, the accustomed movements and gestures, the fixed order of prayers and petitions, the respect for the rubrics, and the like, very often act as veils over the eyes of the worshiper. The routine of the liturgical ceremony can be like an invisible wall separating the consciousness of the worshiper from the explosive power of the mystery of the Liturgy.

Father Harakas' fundamental answer to this problem is as simple as it is true. The words of the Liturgy

[8]*Living the Liturgy*, p. 7.

"beg, require, yes, *demand* participation!" "In peace let us pray to the Lord," the priest calls out to the congregation. With or without a choir, the work of the worshiper at that moment is to collect oneself and actually to turn to the Lord inwardly in prayer saying from the heart, "Lord, have mercy!" This response is not meant to be a routine refrain but a fervent prayer to the living Lord who is present in the Liturgy asking Him to show His loving kindness ("mercy"/*eleos*) toward us right then and there!

Again the priest calls out, "For the peace of God and the salvation of our souls, let us pray to the Lord." The priest is asking the congregation actually to pray for God's peace and for our souls' salvation. The worshiper's work, therefore, is to *pray for them!* Father Harakas suggests that the worshiper turn the words of the priest's calls into brief silent prayers: "O Lord, grant Your peace to all of us gathered here, so that we may worship and glorify You without distraction." Or, "O God, sinner and unworthy though I be, look down upon me in Your mercy and save me." The priest continues: "For peace in the whole world, for the stability of the Churches of God..."The worshiper's work is to pray, "Lord, grant peace to Northern Ireland, Lebanon, Afghanistan...Yes, Lord, show forth your loving kindness to all in the world, so that all people may live in justice and peace." The lips cannot say all these words quickly enough but the mind can pray them many times over as the response "Lord, have mercy" is being chanted by all or by the choir or chanter.

Father Harakas' powerful point is crystal clear. Active participation in the Liturgy means engaging in the work of prayer. The whole Liturgy is a prayer. The worshiper's personal responsibility and work in the Liturgy is to pray to God through the words of the Liturgy. If the choir is singing but not praying at the same time, then the work is not being done. If the congregation is observing, listening, or even singing, but not praying at the same time, then, too, the work is not being done. If the priest is calling out to others to pray, but not himself praying at the same time with them because he is thinking about the order of the service or his sermon, then, again, the real work is not being done. The result is, as Father Harakas puts it, "a rather embarrassing and futile liturgical exercise...NOTHING IS BEING DONE! We have the form of worship and prayer, but no content."[9]

Tragically, this kind of superficiality bordering on blasphemy is the norm rather than the exception for the majority of baptized Orthodox Christians not because they are necessarily acting in bad faith but because they are conditioned even by the ritual itself to be passive participants in worship and they are not alerted, indeed shaken, into being active participants in the Liturgy. Active participation will not become the norm unless it is built on the two foundation stones identified by Father Harakas: (1) the personal responsibility of the worshiper in the Liturgy and (2) the engagement of the worshiper in conscious prayer through the words of the Liturgy. As clergy and laity alike practice these two principles, the "ritual scales", to use Father Harakas' apt expression, fall from their eyes, and they begin to behold the wonders of the treasure of the Liturgy.

By taking personal responsibility and praying the words of the Liturgy, the Liturgy comes alive by the power of the Holy Spirit. The worshipers themselves, participating actively in the work of prayer, are thrilled to discover new insights and experiences in and through the Liturgy. Different words and actions at different times during the Liturgy unexpectedly explode with meaning and power bringing tears to the eyes. Praying the Liturgy means living the Liturgy in its specific prayers, movement, and mystery. The ritual becomes true worship in Spirit and truth. Time seems to hold still, passing before we know it. In Father Harakas' words: "Perhaps it is because in living the Liturgy, we have also entered, if only temporarily, into the Kingdom which is eternal, and which knows no time."[10]

[9]*Living the Liturgy*, p. 75.
[10]*The Melody of Prayer*, pp. 37-38.

5

THEOLOGICAL AND HISTORICAL REFLECTIONS ON THE LITURGY

The Essence of the Liturgy

From its very beginning the Church has been a worshiping Church. When the early Christians gathered together, they met not only for teaching but also for worship and prayer. In particular the Eucharist, the "breaking of bread," has been the central act of Christian worship from earliest times. We read in the Book of Acts: "And they devoted themselves to the apostles' teaching and fellowship, to the breaking of bread and the prayers" (Acts 3:42).

What did the early Christians celebrate through the Eucharist? They celebrated the Christ event—the coming of Christ to the world, His saving ministry, and the presence of God's kingdom in their lives. Jesus proclaimed: "Repent, for the kingdom of heaven is at hand" (Mt. 4:17). The Apostle Peter after Pentecost preached: "Repent, and be baptized, every one of you in the name of Jesus Christ for the forgiveness of your sins; and you shall receive the gift of the Holy Spirit" (Acts 3:38). The Apostle Paul wrote to the Corinthians: "For as often as you eat this bread and drink the cup, you proclaim the Lord's death until He comes" (1 Cor. 11:26). The sacramental life of the Church is a re-living and proclaiming of the good news of salvation in Christ—a sacramental celebration of the gospel.

The Liturgy continues to be the central prayer of the Church and the most profound experience of the joy and power of the gospel. Surrounded by unsurpassed beauty and music, the Liturgy makes present for us here and now the saving work of Christ and all the blessings which flow from it. For these reasons Orthodox thought has tried to express the meaning of the Liturgy through an array of images: a gate to righteousness, a window to heaven, an unceasing celebration of Easter, a continuing Pentecost, a table of God's love, a spiritual banquet, an ephiphany of eternal life, a journey into the kingdom. What are the essential aspects of a theological understanding of the Liturgy?

Christocentric

The focus of the Divine Liturgy is on Christ—His person, birth and adult work, death and resurrection, ascension and glorious return. As a sacrament of Christ the Liturgy is intimately connected to the Church's other great mysteries of initiation, Baptism and Chrismation. In his work *The Life in Christ* Nicholas

Cabasilas, a fourteenth-century theologian, powerfully reminds us that the life in Christ consists of union with the risen Christ and also that Christ is received through all the mysteries of the Church.[1] Baptism is the new birth in Christ, stamping the new Christian with the image of Christ and conferring upon him or her the beginning of Christ-likeness. Chrismation is the energizing of this new life through the dynamic infusion of the Spirit, a divine breath by which we live, move, and have our being in God. The Liturgy, then, according to Cabasilas, is the "final mystery" which sustains and perfects the new life in Christ, a mystery beyond which we cannot go because in the Liturgy Christ offers Himself to us as the bread of life and unites Himself to us more intimately than we are united to our own selves. Writes Cabasilas: "Because of the banquet (that is, the Liturgy) we live with the same life He does."[2]

Christ lives His life through us and molds His features in us through the sacraments of the Church and our willing cooperation with Him. Cabasilas illustrates this truth with a startling image when he says that much as a fetus develops its physical features, for example, its little ears, eyes, nose and lungs, in the mother's womb in order to live an enhanced life after birth, so a Christian, provided that he or she has living faith and is willing to receive Christ through the sacraments, develops his or her Christ-like spiritual features, for example, the capacity to live in communion with God, love, joy and other fruits of the Spirit, in the workshop of this life.

Only in this way can a person acquire the necessary provisions and sensitivities in order to be able to enjoy the fulness of life in God's future kingdom. Christian formation takes place here and now through the action of the risen Christ and by the power of the Spirit. Cabasilas' remarkable Christocentrism is expressed through the following words describing how Christ is present and works in believers whom he calls by the biblical word "saints":

---

[1]Nicholas Cabasilas, *The Life in Christ,* an excellent text for further reading on the Liturgy, as well as on the close relationship between the sacraments and daily living.
[2]Cabasilas, p. 63.

There is nothing of which the saints are in need which He is not Himself. He gives them birth, growth, and nourishment; He is life and breath. By means of Himself He forms an eye for them and, in addition, gives them light and enables them to see Himself. He is the one who feeds and is Himself the food; it is He who provides the bread of life and who is Himself what He provides. He is life for those who live, the sweet odor to those who breathe, the garment for those who would be clothed. Indeed, He is the One who enables us to walk; He Himself is the way, and in addition He is the lodging on the way and its destination...When we must struggle He struggles on our side. For those who are champions in the contest He is the awarder of the prizes; when we are the victors He is the crown of victory.[3]

This centering on Christ comes out at many points during the Divine Liturgy. At the beginning of the Liturgy we sing: "Save us, O Son of God, who rose from the dead!" When the Gospel lesson is read, worshipers receive the words as coming from Christ Himself, and praise Him: "Glory to You, O Lord, glory to You!" When the eucharistic gifts are brought in procession to the altar, we sing: "Let us receive the King of all, invisibly escorted by the angelic hosts." When we receive Holy Communion, we say: "Behold, I approach Christ our immortal King and God."

These and similar expressions show that by faith we perceive the risen and living Christ as the divine celebrant of the Liturgy. He makes His presence known to us as He did to the two disciples walking from Jerusalem to Emmaus after the resurrection when He broke bread with them and set their hearts on fire (Lk. 24:13-32). Christ is in our midst! He is "the Offerer and the Offered, the One who receives and the One who is distributed." He blesses, teaches, forgives and renews us. He offers Himself to us as food and drink for eternal life. The essence of the experience of the eternal Liturgy is thus our life in Christ— our bond of personal com-

[3]Cabasilas, pp. 47-48.

munion with the risen and living Christ which never ends.

Trinitarian

There are petitions and prayers for the forgiveness of sins, but the dominant spirit of the Divine Liturgy is one of joy, doxology and thanksgiving. In its widest vision the Liturgy glorifies the Triune God, Father, Son and Holy Spirit. Accordingly the Liturgy is not only christocentric but trinitarian as well. The Liturgy begins with the invocation: "Blessed is the kingdom of the Father and the Son and the Holy Spirit." All the doxological endings of the various prayers and petitions glorify the Triune God, as for example: "For to You belong all glory, honor and worship, to the Father and the Son and the Holy Spirit, now and forever and to the ages of ages. "At the end of the Liturgy we sing joyously: "We have seen the true light; we have received the heavenly Spirit; we have found the true faith, worshiping the undivided Trinity, for the Trinity has saved us."

Thus, through the Liturgy, the local community of believers are privileged to enter the presence of God. They come before the throne of God as sons and daughters; they have already experienced God"s saving grace, and now they seek to receive it anew. The Spirit leads them to sing of all that God has done in salvation history, and especially through Jesus' ministry, to save them. They offer honor and worship to the Father, the Son and the Holy Spirit. Moved by awe and wonder before the majesty and holiness of God, they sing: "Holy, holy, holy, Lord Sabaoth; heaven and earth are filled with Your glory."

As they pray fervently, Christian worshipers are lifted beyond time into a celebration of the mystery of the eternal kingdom, God's sovereign rule embracing past, present and future. They remember the saints of all times and places. They are united with the angels in the praise and glorification of God. By faith they catch a glimpse of the eternal liturgy in the heavenly Jerusalem, the celebration of the marriage feast of the Lamb and His Bride, when pain and death will be no more, but all things will be new (Rev. 21:1-5).

However, the Liturgy is neither an escape from the world nor does it ignore the world. We gather together in the Liturgy in order to renew our vision of both our identity and vocation as Orthodox Christians living in contemporary society. We "commit ourselves and one another and our whole life to Christ." We bind ourselves by solemn prayers to love one another and to lead lives of holiness in the world. We also make bold to intercede for the world, for peace and unity, for the poor and the oppressed, for the sick and the captive. No one and nothing is excluded from the vision of the Liturgy.

In the Liturgy we ask for and receive the grace of the Holy Spirit. We pray to the Father: "Send down Your Holy Spirit upon us and upon these gifts." One of the benefits of partaking of the consecrated Gifts is "communion of the Holy Spirit." We also sing: "We have seen the true light; we have received the heavenly Spirit!" Thus the Liturgy is an ongoing experience of Pentecost, and Pentecost means mission, witness, sharing our faith. Having received the grace of the Spirit we are energized to go out to proclaim Christ's good news to all. Inspired by a new sense of who we are as Orthodox Christians, we are also empowered to carry out our various callings in the world; to discharge our many responsibilities at work, school, office, home, neighborhood and public life. For Orthodox Christians there is "a liturgy after the Liturgy," a mission of love and service in the world, a divine calling to be Christ's hands and feet, His eyes and voice, for all our brothers and sisters everywhere. Thus the Liturgy leads us to become new martyrs (the original meaning of this word is witness)— to give witness before the world that we are citizens of God's kingdom and bearers of a new quality of life by the grace of Christ. In so doing we fulfill Jesus' challenging words that Christians are to be, by deeds as well as words, the light of the world and the salt of the earth.

The Names of the Liturgy

Lord's Supper

The Divine Liturgy has received many titles in Christian tradition which express the basic theological themes of the Liturgy. The first among them is *kyriakon deipnon* (1 Cor. 11:20), which literally means "Dominical Supper," and is commonly translated "Lord's Supper." According to St. Paul the sacramental meal which the Corinthian Christians were celebrating as a Church around 51 A.D. was the Lord's, that is, it had been established by Jesus Himself on the night when He was betrayed and had the same significance as the Last Supper which Jesus celebrated with His disciples. Since St. Paul's words are the first report of how the early Christians celebrated the Liturgy, they are worth quoting at length:

> For I received from the Lord what I also delivered to you, that the Lord Jesus on the night when He was betrayed took bread, and when He had given thanks, He broke it, and said, "This is my body which is for you. Do this in remembrance of me." In the same way also the cup, after supper, saying, "This cup is the new covenant in my blood. Do this, as often as you drink it, in remembrance of me." For as often as you eat this bread and drink the cup, you proclaim the Lord's death until He comes. Whoever, therefore eats the bread or drinks the cup of the Lord in an unworthy manner will be guilty of profaning the body and blood of the Lord. Let each person examine one self, and so eat of the bread and drink of the cup (1 Cor. 11:23-28).

St. Paul's account of the Lord's Supper shows several important aspects about the meaning of the Liturgy in its earliest form. One is that whether St. Paul received this rite directly from the risen Christ at the time of the Damascus event or from the other Apostles who had earlier received it from Christ (St. Paul's words are not clear on this matter), the origins of the Liturgy go back to Jesus Himself. St. Paul views the Liturgy as a tradition handed down since the days of Jesus and as a central part of the life of the early Church. What the Corinthians were celebrating as the Lord's Supper was a continuation of the Last Supper. Just as the twelve disciples had gathered around Jesus to share a solemn meal with Him on the night before His death, so also the Corinthian Christians continued to gather around the Lord's table to share a sacred rite of the same significance. Since this rite was celebrated frequently, probably weekly, it shows that the Church was a Church of the Liturgy from the beginning.

Another important point made by the above passage is that the Lord's Supper is directly connected with Christ's sacrifice on the cross as a saving event. Jesus' solemn words and actions, namely, the breaking of bread and the pouring out of wine, as well as His words of institution ("This is my body" and so on), had pointed to Christ's impending death as a sacrifice "for the forgiveness of sins" (Mt. 26:28). So, too, for St. Paul, the sacramental actions and words of the Lord's Supper proclaim Christ's saving death as the basis of "the new covenant" (1 Cor. 11:25). The word "remembrance" (*anamnesis*) as used in 1 Cor. 11:25 signifies not merely an abstract calling to mind but rather a sacramental reliving of the once for all death of Christ, a reliving not only of Jesus' death but also His resurrection, because the crucified and risen Christ cannot be separated. Therefore, those who share in the Lord's Supper, a continuation of the Last Supper, participate sacramentally in the person and mission of Christ, especially the central events of His death and resurrection, and they also enjoy the blessings which flow from these saving events.

A final important matter indicated by St. Paul is the partaking of Holy Communion. Christ had said to His disciples "This is my body" and "This is my blood" (Mt. 26:26-27). Elsewhere He had declared: "He who eats my flesh and drinks my blood has eternal life...{and} abides in me, and I in him" (Jn 6:54, 56). Partaking of the consecrated gifts is partaking of Christ, a total and abiding union with Him. St. Paul also writes: "Whoever...eats the bread or drinks the cup of the Lord" partakes of "the body and blood of the Lord," and should do so, therefore, worthily (1 Cor. 11:27-28), that is, with a deep personal awareness of the meaning of the Lord's Supper and sincere commitment to its implications for daily living. If we are united with Christ through Holy Communion in the Liturgy, we must also be united with Him in daily life, showing evidence of Christ-like qualities in all aspects of our living. Otherwise we are judged guilty of profaning the sacrament, indeed Christ Himself.

A word of explanation about the nature of Holy Communion may be helpful. the bold words "body and blood of the Lord" should not be understood in a grossly materialistic way, as if one were to look under a microscope for—heaven forbid—physical tissue and corpuscles in the pure body and precious blood of the Lord. The Lord's Supper is a sacramental communion which by the power of the Holy Spirit effects a true and personal union with the risen and living Christ. The Church Fathers have never tried to analyze exactly *how* Christ is present in the consecrated gifts but strongly affirmed *that* He was fully present. They took Him at His word, "This is my body" and "This is my blood" (Mt. 26:26-27; Mk 14:22, 24), nothing more, nothing less. Through Holy Communion we partake of Christ in His full, personal presence. But the change of the gifts of bread and wine into the body and blood of Christ by the Holy Spirit is mystical (*mystike*) and sacramental (*mysteriake*), not physical, because after the consecration we still taste the qualities of ordinary bread and wine. Holy Communion is, therefore, a great mystery of grace and faith, a sacramental eating and drinking. The Lord's Supper, just as the Last Supper, is truly a mystical supper (*mystikos deipnos*) in which we partake of the risen Christ and His glorified humanity, a divine union which cleanses and glorifies us by grace (*theosis*).

Love Feast

Among the early Christians the celebrations of the Liturgy, which were part of a full meal, were also called *agapai*— "love feasts." *Agape* signifies a special quality of love, a love which reflects God's love, pure and outgoing, selfless and sacrificial. Christ made this kind of love central to His teaching (Mt. 5:44; 22:37-39; Lk. 10:29-37). St. Paul defined it as the fulfilment of the Law (Rm. 13:10) and the greatest gift of the Spirit (1 Cor. 13). A study of the verb *agapan* ("to love") and its derivatives shows that Christians, as no others, developed the language of love to an amazing degree based on their experience of God's love through Christ (Jn 3:16).

It is not surprising, therefore, that the early Christians used the word *agape* to name their weekly common meals in which they celebrated the Lord's Supper. Although the Lord's Supper was later separated from these full meals because of abuses (1 Cor. 11:20; Jd. 12), it is important for us to continue to view the Liturgy as an *agape*, a love feast of brothers and sisters united by the holy love of Christ.

To think of the Liturgy as a love feast is to think of the Last Supper. St. John the beloved disciple describes the Last Supper most clearly as a love feast. As Jesus sat at table with His disciples, His heart was full of love for them, including Judas who tragically abandoned this first love feast. In the words of St. John the Evangelist, Jesus "loved His own who were in the world, He loved them to the end" (Jn 13:1). Divine love motivated Jesus to wash the disciples' feet as an example of humility and service. By sharing the Last Supper as well as living words of truth with His disciples (Jn chaps.. 13-17), Jesus shared Himself as love. One of the main themes of Jesus's last discourse to the disciples was love: "A new commandment I give to you, that you love one another; even as I have loved you, that you also love one another" (Jn 13:34-35). And

again: "As the Father has loved me, so have I loved you; abide in my love...Greater love has no one than this, that one lay down one's life for one's friends" (Jn 15:9, 13).

Jesus' words of love resound in the Divine Liturgy: "Let us love one another that with one mind we may confess...Father, Son, and Holy Spirit." In the Liturgy we as beloved disciples approach the Lord's table which is a table of love to partake of the food of angels, the bread of love, Christ Himself. A table of God's love, the Divine Liturgy is a communal love feast of the Church as the body of Christ which unites believers with Christ and with each other as brothers and sisters, breaking down all class, race and sex barriers. The power of divine love manifests the new humanity in Christ and gives the most convincing evidence that we are His followers: "By this all will now that you are my disciples, if you have love for one another" (Jn 13:35).

Eucharist

An important feature of Jewish meals, especially those held on major feasts such as the Passover, was the giving of thanks to God not only as Creator and provider of all good things but also as Savior and deliverer of His people in history through great saving acts such as the exodus from Egypt. We find that Jesus continued this tradition of offering prayers of thanksgiving to God at meals. When He fed the multitudes in the wilderness, He gave thanks prior to the breaking and distribution of the loaves (Mk 8:6; Jn 6:11, 23). At the Last Supper Jesus again gave thanks (*eucharistesas*) before breaking the bread and offering the cup to the disciples (Lk. 22:17, 19). Jesus' act of giving thanks at the Last Supper became a central part of the Liturgy. We note that the Corinthian Christians offered many prayers of thanksgiving (*eucharistia*) when they celebrated the Lord's Supper and other fellow Christians affirmed them by saying the "amen" (1 Cor. 14:16). Within a few generations the Liturgy itself came to be called Eucharist (*Eucharistia*) or Thanksgiving.

One of the most valuable historical sources about the Liturgy is the ancient Christian writing known as *The Didache*. Composed around the turn of the second century, this document contains instructions about the celebration of the Liturgy which it calls "Eucharist". *The Didache* also includes actual prayers of thanksgiving offered by early Christians which are both profound and inspiring:

> Regarding the Eucharist (*eucharistia*). Give thanks (*eucharistesate*) as follows: First, concerning the cup.[4] "We give You thanks (*eucharistoumen*), our Father, for the holy vine of David Your servant, which You have made known to us through Your servant Jesus. To You be the glory for evermore." Next,

[4]Some early Christian traditions feature the offering of the cup first and the breaking of the bread second, a sequence reflected in Lk. 22:17-19.

concerning the broken bread. "We give You thanks, our Father, for the life and knowledge You have made known to us through Jesus Your servant. To You be the glory for evermore. As this broken bread was scattered over the hills and then, when gathered, became one (loaf), so may Your Church be gathered from the ends of the earth into Your kingdom. For Yours is the glory and power through Jesus Christ for evermore."

(Didache 9.1-4)

Accordingly one of the main themes of the Liturgy is thanksgiving. The frequent use of the title "Eucharist" for the Liturgy is a constant reminder of the theme of thanksgiving. The main prayer of consecration is also often called the great Eucharistic Prayer, initiated by the priest's call to the congregation: "Let us give thanks to the Lord." In this prayer we give thanks to God for all creation, for His kingdom, the Holy Spirit, the Liturgy itself, and especially for His Son and what God has done for us through Christ. It is at this time that we also sing *Se Imnoumen*, the most solemn prayer of praise and thanksgiving: "We praise You, we bless you, we give thanks to You...Lord our God." There are other references to thanksgiving in the Liturgy as well. St. Ephraem the Syrian said that praise and thanksgiving lengthen our earthly lifespans by giving them a heavenly quality.[5] The Eucharist sanctifies our earthly existence and makes it eternal by the bestowal of God's grace. As the central sacrament of the Church, it helps us to "give thanks in all circumstances" (1 Thess. 5:16) and to transform each day into a prayer of thanksgiving.

Liturgy

The most prevalent name for the sacrament of the Eucharist is Liturgy. The word "Liturgy" translates the Greek word *leitourgia* deriving from two words *leitos* (people) and *ergon* (work) and therefore meaning a work of the people or a work for the people. Among the ancient Greeks the word *leitourgia* denoted a public

---

[5]S. Ephraem (d. 373 AD) was the greatest theologian-poet among the Church Fathers. See Sebastian Brock, *The Harp of the Spirit* (St. Alban and St. Sergius, 1983).

service or act, including an act of worship of deity, performed for the benefit of all. In the Jewish and Christian traditions this word was used in a similar way. For example, in the New Testament this word can denote an act of service to others, whether spiritual (Phil. 2:17) or material (2 Cor. 9:12), or also an act of worship (Lk. 1:23; Acts 13:2; Heb. 9:21). In later Christian tradition the liturgical application prevailed and by the fourth century the title "Liturgy" had become the most common name of the sacrament of the Eucharist.

Why is the Liturgy a work of the people? Jesus' conversation about the miracle of the feeding of the multitudes, which according to the Church Fathers prefigures the Eucharist, gives us an insight into the meaning of the eucharistic sacrament which we call "Liturgy". When Jesus fed the multitude in the wilderness, He intended this miracle as a messianic sign showing that He himself was the heavenly bread. But misunderstanding the meaning of the miracle, many were merely satisfied by having eaten their fill and were looking to acclaim Jesus an earthly king who would continuously fulfil their physical needs. Jesus then challenged them not to work (*ergazesthe*) for perishable but eternal food. When they asked what they must so in order to be doing the works of God, Jesus replied: "This is the work (*ergon*) of God, that you believe in Him whom He has sent" (Jn 6:26-29).

To believe in Jesus as the Christ of God, and all that this faith necessarily implies, is doing the true work of God. For Jesus faith is not only an intellectual acceptance of the truth that He is the Christ of God but also a total commitment to a way of life of which He is the supreme model. Jesus had said to His disciples: "My food is to do the will of Him who sent me, and to accomplish His work" (Jn 4:34). Jesus' whole life was based on but one primary principle, love of God; it was inspired by but one purpose, to accomplish God's saving work; and it had but one goal, the glory of God.

The Divine Liturgy is truly the work of the people of God because through the Liturgy we live our faith in Christ and we celebrate God's saving work not only in the history of salvation but also as a present reality among us. As an act of worship of the living Triune God, Father, Son and Holy Spirit, the Liturgy is the work of all the people of God requiring the prayerful attention, energy, and active participation by all. Almost all of the petitions, prayers, and hymns of the Liturgy offered by the priest are formulated in the first personal plural("Let us pray to the Lord; Let us commit ourselves...and our whole life to Christ our God;" and "To You we offer glory"); they invite the active participation of all.

The Liturgy is a dialogue not only between the people and the priest, but also between the whole congregation and God. The essence of the Liturgy as a spiritual event is this dynamic, personal interaction of God and His people, which transforms the Liturgy from a formal rite into a fervent prayer glowing with living faith and the awesome presence of God. As the work of the people praising and worshiping God, the Liturgy then becomes worship "in Spirit and truth" (Jn 4:23), and the key to the meaning of the whole mystery of life. It reveals the new creation in Christ and confers Christ-likeness upon us. It empowers believers by the Holy Spirit to carry out God's mission and to witness to it by a new way of life. The Liturgy itself becomes the chief sign of the transfiguration of all life and creation. Thus the work of the people in worshiping God is intimately connected to the work of the people in serving God's purposes in all areas of life for the glory of God.

The Historical Growth and Structure of the Liturgy

Historical Development

The early Christians celebrated the Liturgy as the most important part of their life together according to the command of Jesus: "Do this in remembrance of me" (Lk. 22:19; 1 Co. 11:24-25). During the first and second generations of Christians the Liturgy was celebrated as part of a full meal which was held in the evening (1 Cor. 11). On the basis of St. Paul's accounts of the gatherings of the Church of Corinth in First Corinthians chapters 11 and 14[e], we can infer that this meal was informal and that the worship was free and spontaneous. Writes St. Paul: "When you come together, each one has a hymn, a lesson, a revelation, a tongue, or an interpretation" (1 Cor. 14:26).

[e]A small number of scholars think that these two chapters are accounts of two different Church gatherings, one a communion service and the other a service of praise and teaching. However, St. Paul in 1 Cor. 15:2 seems to indicate one weekly gathering which combined all elements of Christian worship.

But human weaknesses resulted also in irregularities, abuses, and dissensions (1 Cor. 11:18, 21; 14:23, 33). St. Paul did not wish to eliminate spontaneity but to order it: "Let all things be done for edification" (1 Cor. 14:26) and again "all thing should be done decently and in order" (1 Cor. 14:40).

Our next historical source for the conduct of the Liturgy is *The Didache*, dating from about the beginning of the second century, which evidences continued spontaneity in Christian worship but also greater concern for order as well. Because of practical difficulties, the Liturgy had already been separated from the common meal which is not mentioned by *The Didache* in connection with the Eucharist. But *The Didache* (chaps. 9-10 and 14) gives explicit instructions about the celebration of the Liturgy. Christians were to assemble together on the Lord's Day (Sunday). They were to offer a confession of sins, quite possible through a set prayer, prior to the solemn breaking of the bread in the Eucharist. They were also to offer specific prayers of thanksgiving. No one quarreling with a fellow Christian was to participate in the eucharistic gathering unless first reconciled. Unbaptized persons were, of course, expressly excluded from receiving the Eucharist. *The Didache*, too, makes clear that the Christian leaders, called *episkopoi* (bishops or presbyters), *diakonoi* (deacons) and *prophetai* (prophets) took the initiative in leading the worship and the celebration of the Eucharist.

By the middle of the second century the continuing development of the Liturgy had resulted in a more formal type of Liturgy without excluding spontaneous elements altogether. Our witness for this period is St. Justin Martyr who provides detailed information about the conduct of the Liturgy in his *First Apology*, chapters 65-67.

According to St. Justin, the Liturgy began with readings from the Gospels or the Old Testament Prophets, followed by a sermon which was preached by the Church leader called *proestos* (president) interpreting the readings and applying them to life. Prayers then were offered for Christians and the world. The exchange of the kiss of peace took place. The central act of the Liturgy was the Eucharist when bread, wine and water were brought to the Church leader who offered the prayer of consecration. This prayer was an established prayer, and probably included Jesus' words of institution, but the leader had the freedom to expand the prayer with his own words while the congregation responded with the "amen". After the consecration the deacons distributed the eucharistic gifts to those present and also brought them to those absent for serious reasons. The Liturgy ended with the collection of a free will offering for the poor, sick, prisoners, visitors and others who needed help.

The above examples indicate the historical growth of the Liturgy from a simple liturgical act to a more complicated structure, from spontaneous prayers, hymns, and teachings to fixed forms of worship. A similar development took place in the case of the sacrament of Baptism and other aspects of Church life such as Church offices. For instance, during the second century, the tradition became quite clear that the chief celebrant of the Liturgy was the bishop, or a presbyter appointed by the bishop, while the deacons served as designated assistants. These developments do not come as a surprise. They are part of the historical and incarnational life of the Church establishing norms of unity and appropriately adapting to ongoing needs and circumstances by the inspiration and guidance of the Holy Spirit.

We need not pursue further the development of the Liturgy in its historical complexity.[7] Different liturgical patterns evolved in various Churches of the East and the West. They were all based on the Last Supper and on local Christian traditions of celebrating the Liturgy.

With regard to the Churches in the East, several main Liturgies were eventually established. The Liturgy of the Church of Jerusalem became known as the Liturgy of St. James, the first bishop of Jerusalem. The Church of Alexandria developed its own form of the

---

[7]For further reading see A. Schemann, *Introduction to Liturgical Theology* (St. Vladimir's Seminary Press, 1966); Gregory Dix, *The Shape of the Liturgy* (A. & C. Black, 1945, reprinted by Harper and Row); C. Jones, G. Wainwright and E. Yarnold, eds., *The Study of the Liturgy* (Oxford University Press, 1978); W. Rordorf and others, *The Eucharist of the Early Christians* (Pueblo, 1978); R. Kevin Seasoltz, *Living Bread, Saving Cup: Readings on the Eucharist* (Collegeville, 1982); Robert Taft, *The Great Entrance* (Rome, 1975); T. J. Talley, *The Origins of the Liturgical Year* (Pueblo, 1986).

Liturgy known as the Liturgy of St. Mark, the follower of the Apostles Paul and Peter, who was regarded by tradition as the founder of the Church of Alexandria. Another Liturgy under the name of St. Gregory the Theologian was used in Cappadocia, the homeland of St. Gregory, but also in Alexandria.

The Church of Constantinople developed its own Liturgy known as the Liturgy of St. Basil which it used as its main Liturgy until about the twelfth century. Now the Liturgy of St. Basil is celebrated only ten times a year on the following days: the Feast of St. Basil which is on January 1; on the Vigils of Christmas, Epiphany and Pascha; on the five Sundays of Great Lent, and on Holy Thursday. After the twelfth century the Church of Constantinople replaced the regular use of the Liturgy of St. Basil with the use of a shorter and simplified version known as the Liturgy of St. John Chrysostom, which in earlier times had probably served as the weekday Liturgy of Constantinople. It should be noted that scholars are uncertain about the exact connections of these apostolic figures and great Church Fathers with the Liturgies which bear their names, but all agree that these Liturgies had a long historical development in the local Churches in which they were established.

Another Liturgy that should be mentioned is the Liturgy of the Pre-Sanctified Gifts. This is not a full Liturgy because it lacks the prayer of consecration, the eucharistic Gifts having been consecrated on the previous Sunday. A solemn service bearing a character befitting the spirit of Lent, the Liturgy of the Pre-Sanctified Gifts was developed in the Church of Constantinople and eventually came to be used on Wednesdays and Fridays of the Great Lent and also on the first three days of Holy Week, which is the present practice. Constantinople was the center of Orthodoxy and a crucible for liturgical development. Under the influence of the Church of Constantinople all the Orthodox Churches came to use the Liturgies of St. John Chrysostom, St. Basil and the Pre-Sanctified Liturgy according to the Constantinopolitan pattern which now prevails. The other Liturgies of St. James, St. Mark and St. Gregory may be celebrated in the Orthodox Churches on the feast days of these saints.

Present Structure

The current form of the Liturgy of St. John Chrysostom is the result of centuries of liturgical development. Its basic structure, however, goes back to ancient times and is determined by two fundamental liturgical acts, the reading of Scripture and the offering of the eucharistic Gifts. The reading of Scripture and the homily which followed it were Jewish liturgical customs practiced in the synagogues which the early Christians continued as part of their own worship. The offering of the eucharistic gifts, that is, the Eucharist itself, although having certain connections with the Passover meal by way of the Last Supper, is a unique Christian institution. These two liturgical acts, highlighted by solemn entrances or processions, still shape the present form of the Liturgy, with the addition of many petitions, prayers, hymns, and liturgical gestures, which over centuries came to make up the total Liturgy with its beauty, simplicity and dignity.

An important development was the separation of the preparation of the bread and wine from the eucharistic part of the Liturgy and the creation of a distinct preparatory service conducted prior to the public celebration of the Liturgy. This service of preparation is called *Proskomide* (literally, "bringing forth gifts") and is conducted by the priest during Matins or even before Matins on the left side altar called the *Prothesis* (Table of Preparation or Presentation). Although little known to and usually unseen by the congregation, a fact in many ways unfortunate, the *Proskomide* is still an integral part of the Liturgy. Thus the present structure of the Liturgy features three main parts which, together with their elaborations, can be outlined as follows:

A. The Preparation of the Gifts (*Proskomide*)

    1. Priest's Prayers of Preparation (*Kairos*)
    2. Priest's Vesting
    3. Service of Preparation of the Gifts (*Proskomide*)
       a. Cutting of Particles from the Offering Bread (*Prosphoron*)
       b. Commemorations of Saints and the faithful (living and dead).

        c. Covering of the Gifts
        d. A Prayer of Blessing

  B. The Liturgy of the Word

     1. Doxological Invocation
     2. Great Litany
     3. Antiphons
     4. Small Entrance
     5. Trisagion
     6. Biblical Readings
     7. Sermon

  C. The Eucharist

     1. The Cherubic Hymn and Great Entrance
     2. Petitions
     3. Kiss of Peace
     4. The Creed
     5. The Offering of the Gifts (*Anaphora*)
        a. Thanksgiving
        b. Trisagion ("Holy, holy, holy, Lord Sabaoth")
        c. Words of Institution
        d. Offering of the Gifts
        e. Epiclesis and Consecration
        f. Commemorations
     6. Petitions and the Lord's Prayer
     7. Bowing of the Head
     8. Preparation of the Consecrated Gifts and Holy Communion
     9. Hymns and Prayers of Thanksgiving
    10. The Dismissal

In its totality the Divine Liturgy is a complex but harmonious whole of verbal aspects and dramatic actions. The verbal aspects consist of doxologies, thanksgivings, readings, petitions, confessions, intercessions, invitations, hymns, prayers, and professions of faith. The dramatic actions include processions, acts of blessing, the kiss of peace, Holy Communion, censing, and the giving of the blessed bread (*antidoron*).

The Liturgy is like a diamond sculpted in a fine setting of liturgical actions, hymns and prayers. A harmonious unity of movement, music and prayer, the Liturgy is celebrated against the rich background of

Orthodox sacred art and architecture, and inspires the whole person, body and soul. Through the Divine Liturgy the people of God experience by visible means the invisible beauty of heaven.

However, we should not remain with only the external beauty of the Liturgy which can stir feelings of awe similar to those accomplished by an impressive opera. The deep mystery of the Liturgy is the mystery of the presence of God, the Father, the Son, and the Holy Spirit. The text and ceremony of the Liturgy come alive by the energizing and transforming presence of God who makes Himself known to a congregation of prayerful, repentant and loving hearts.

Then the Liturgy becomes an experience of the new humanity and the local parish reveals its identity, the fulness of life of the One, Holy, Catholic, and Apostolic Church. The new creation in Christ is manifest and the destructive powers of sin, death and Satan are defeated. The Liturgy is an epiphany of the Kingdom and the source of a new quality of life which graces all things in creation.

6

HOW TO USE THIS STUDY

Two Session Program

This Study Guide provides practical guidance, as well as theological background, for the study of the Liturgy in connection with the video film "The Divine Liturgy of St. John Chrysostym." Chapters 1-3 can be used by group leaders or teachers as the actual text in presenting the video to a group. What follows in this Chapter provides suggestions about specific programs and discussion questions for up to twelve sessions in an extended study of the Liturgy.

Since the video consists of two half-hour parts, the basic program involves two sessions. At the first session begin with Chapter 1 of the Study Guide, "Preparing to View the Video," as introductory remarks. These introductory remarks, which will take from twelve to fifteen minutes, can be used in whole or in part. After showing the first part of the video, about fifteen or twenty minutes will remain for discussion if an hour has been scheduled for the first session. Proceed with discussion on the basis of the first two paragraphs of Chapter 2, "The Liturgy of the Word," including the discussion questions which are repeated here:

1. What are your own impressions about what you saw and heard?

2. If you were to choose one or two main points to talk about, what would they be? Why?

3. Did you learn some new things about the Liturgy? What are they?

4. What did you think of the seminarians speaking about their difficulties in concentrating and actively participating during the Liturgy?

5. How can these difficulties be dealt with?

6. Now that you have seen the first half of the video, how would you define the Liturgy? What would you say the Liturgy is all about?

7. In what ways do you connect the Liturgy with your life?

If up to ninety minutes are allowed for the first session, a brief break of about ten to fifteen minutes is advisable after the video is shown, to be followed by discussion. If more than ninety minutes can be scheduled, then there would be time (twenty minutes or more) for small group discussions (consisting of five persons or more) gathering in circles in the same hall or going to separate rooms. For instance:

Introduction— 12-15 minutes
Part 1 of video— 30 minutes
Break— 10-15 minutes
Small group discussion— 20-40 minutes
Reports from small groups— 3 minutes each
General discussion— 10-20 minutes

In the case of small group discussions, a facilitator and a recorder should be chosen for each group. Also, copies of the questions should be made available to all participants with adequate space for writing answers.

At the second session begin with the showing of part 2 of the video. Discussion may then follow on the basis of the first three paragraphs of Chapter 3 of the Study Guide, "The Eucharist," including these questions:

1. Having heard the explanations of the second part of the video, what would you say is the essence of the Eucharist? How would you define the Eucharist?

2. What are the highlights or most inspiring moments of the Eucharist for you? Why?

3. What do we need to celebrate the Eucharist with special care and concentration?

4. Do you have any questions about what you saw and heard in the video?

5. How do you relate the Eucharist to daily life?

6. Is the Eucharist truly a thanksgiving for you? For what things are you thankful to God?

7. In what various ways can we express our gratitude to God? How is it possible, in St. Paul's words, to "give thanks in *all circumstances*" (1 Thess. 5:18)?

If more than sixty minutes are scheduled for the second session, follow the instructions regarding small groups and breaks given above under the first session.

One-Day Retreat

For a one-day retreat on the Divine Liturgy the following program is suggested:

8:30–9:30 a.m.	Celebration of the Divine Liturgy
9:30–10:25 a.m.	Registration and Breakfast
10:15 a.m.	Introduction to the video
10:30 a.m.	Part 1 of the video
11:00–11:45 a.m.	Small groups
11:45–12:30 p.m.	Small group reports and general discussion
12:30 –1:15 p.m.	Lunch
1:15 p.m.	Christian hymns and songs
1:30 p.m.	Part 2 of the video
2:00–2:45 p.m.	Small groups
2:45 p.m.	Coffee break
3:00–3:45 p.m.	Small group reports and general discussion
3:45 p.m.	Closing hymn and prayer

If the retreat is an overnight retreat, a similar pattern can be followed for additional evening or day sessions. In terms of content, one or more of the subsections of Chapters 2 and 3 may be used, including the relevant discussion questions given below.

Multiple Session Program

It is possible on the basis of this Study Guide to offer instruction on the Divine Liturgy over an extended period of time or during a particular liturgical season such as the pre-Christmas Lent. A priest, for example, could choose to offer a series of sermons on the Liturgy utilizing the ten sub-sections of Chapters 2 and 3. Or a series of talks could be given to an adult study group which may meet either Sunday morning after the Liturgy or during the week. Or a mature young adult/ high school group could be challenged to study the Liturgy more deeply over a period of time.

In such cases two sessions should be devoted to the viewing of the two parts of the video at their appropriate time and according to the instructions given above under "Two Sessions". Beyond these two sessions the sub-sections of Chapters 2 and 3 can serve as the basic material for additional sessions. At the discretion of the group leader or teacher, one or two sub-sections can be used for each session, depending on how many sessions are scheduled. If the schedule is limited, some of the subsections can be entirely omitted. If on the other hand a schedule of more than twelve sessions is possible, the longer sub-sections such as that on the Lord's Prayer can be treated in two or more sessions. A creative Christian educator can develop new sessions on the basis of individual prayers, petitions, and hymns of the Liturgy which may not be treated adequately or may not be treated at all in this Study Guide.

The two parts of the video can be shown more than once to the same group. For example, part 1 can be shown at the first session and again at the sixth session when the topic "Applications of the Liturgy" is discussed (see sub-section 5 of Chapter 2). Similarly, part 2 can be shown at the seventh and again at the twelfth session. Obviously particular segments of the video can be briefly shown at any session as it is relevant. For example, the video segment on the Great Entrance can be shown at the session devoted to the Great Entrance. However, the sensitive group leader or teacher will be mindful not to be excessively dependent on the film. After an adequate exposure to the video or any parts of it, the educational challenge lies in generating people's response not merely to the video but to the Liturgy itself as the center of weekly living.

Discussion Questions   Discussion questions have been given above under the "Two Session Program". What follows are discussion questions for each of the sub-sections of Chapters 2 and 3. The group leader or teacher can also raise or allow participants to raise other questions for discussion. The group leader or teacher should be prepared for discussion by carefully viewing the video ahead of time and taking notes, by reading with understanding the Study Guide, and by consulting the bibliography given at the end of the Study Guide.

The Meaning of the Liturgy

1. The video described the Liturgy as "a jewel among the treasures of Orthodox worship".

What does this mean to you? Is it true for you? Why or why not?

2. What specific parts, prayers, or hymns of the liturgy remind you that Christ Himself is the precious jewel of the Liturgy?

3. How can we enliven our awareness that the Liturgy is "our personal meeting with the risen Christ"?

4. How is the Liturgy related to the good news of the gospel? Why is the Liturgy "evangelical"?

5. How and when is the Liturgy an "Emmaus experience" for you?

6. How would you sum up the "theology" of the Liturgy?

7. Study the first mystical prayer of the Liturgy given below:

"Lord, our God, whose power is beyond compare, and glory is beyond understanding; whose mercy is boundless, and love for us is ineffable: look upon us and upon this holy house in Your compassion. Grant to us and to those who pray with us Your abundant mercy."

What are the attributes of God? What is our appeal to God? On what basis do we make it? What feelings and thoughts toward God does this prayer inspire?

Preparations for the Liturgy

1. In what sense is the Liturgy God's call, a ringing of a spiritual bell, to us?

2. Why do we need to be prepared to hear and to heed God's call through the Liturgy?

3. Name and discuss specific ways in which the priest prepares for the Liturgy.

4. Name and discuss specific ways you can prepare for the Liturgy.

5. What factors keep people from preparing for the Liturgy? What factors can motivate a person to prepare for the Liturgy?

6. Read the following prayer offered by the priest as he washes his hands and prepares to conduct the Proskomide Service (Preparation of the Gifts):

"I shall wash my hands in innocence, O Lord, and shall serve before Your altar. I shall listen to the voice of Your praise and declare all Your wonders. Lord, I have loved the beauty of Your house, the place where Your glory abides. Destroy not my soul with sinners, nor my life with men of blood in whose hands are transgressions; their right hand is full of bribes. But as for me, I have walked in innocence. Redeem me, O Lord, and have mercy on me. My foot is set upon the straight path; in the assemblies, O Lord, I shall bless You."

What commitments to God does the priest make through this prayer? What does he ask of God? How do these commitments and requests apply to lay Orthodox Christians?

Active Participation in the Liturgy

1. What is the difference between passive and active participation in the Liturgy? When are you a passive or active participant?

2. Why was the Liturgy never meant to be a "spectator event"?

3. Leitourgia means "work of the people". What is the work of the people, and your work, in the Liturgy? What are the requirements and benefits of this work?

4. Name and discuss specific ways the Liturgy itself both demands and helps us to participate actively.

5. What does it mean "to pray the Liturgy" and to establish an "active presence" at the Liturgy?

6. How do you participate actively in the Liturgy?

7. What would you say to someone who complains: "I don't get anything out of the Liturgy"?

8. Study the following mystical prayer offered at the beginning of the Liturgy:

"Lord, You have given us grace to offer these common prayers with one heart. You have promised to grant the requests of two or three gathered in Your name. Fulfil now the petitions of Your servants for our benefit, giving us the knowledge of Your truth in this world, and granting us eternal life in the world to come."

Who gives us grace to participate actively in the Liturgy? What is Christ's promise to us when we gather in His name? What requests do we make to Christ through this prayer? What feelings and thoughts does this prayer inspire?

Content of the Liturgy of the Word

1. Describe and discuss the purpose, procedure, and significance of the Proskomide Service according to the video. How can the laity participate in this Service?

2. Define and discuss the meaning of the titles "Liturgy of the Catechumens", "Synaxis", and "Liturgy of the Word". How does each of these titles apply to our situation today?

3. Why is it extremely important to come early for the beginning of the Liturgy and to be present for the whole Liturgy?

4. What is the kingdom of God? How is the doxological blessing, "Blessed is the kingdom of the Father and the Son and the Holy Spirit", related to the petitions of the Great Litany and the rest of the Liturgy? What connections do you draw between God's kingdom and your life?

5. Explain the origins and meaning of the Trisagion; and discuss its application in our lives.

6. What does Scripture say about God's Word? How does the Liturgy highlight the importance of God's Word? How can people be encouraged to hear, read, and apply God's Word?

7. Read the following prayer offered by the priest at the end of the Proskomide Service:

"O God, our God, You sent the heavenly Bread, the food for the whole world, our Lord and God Jesus Christ, as Savior, Redeemer, and Benefactor, to bless us and sanctify us. Do bless this offering and accept it upon Your heavenly altar. As a good and loving God remember those who brought it and those for whom it was brought. Keep us blameless in the celebration of Your Divine Mysteries. For sanctified and glorified is Your most honorable and majestic name, of the Father and the Son and the Holy Spirit, now and forever and to the ages of ages. Amen."

How is Christ described in this prayer? What do we ask of God? What feelings and thoughts does this prayer inspire?

Applications of the Liturgy

1. Give specific examples from the first part of the Liturgy and discuss how the Liturgy is related to daily life.

2. How do you connect the "work" of the Liturgy with your job or present occupation?

3. How do you connect the Liturgy with recreation?

4. How do you connect the Liturgy with your family, friendships, and personal issues and problems?

5. Who makes it possible to experience a natural continuity between the Liturgy and daily life? Why and how?

6. When and how do the Liturgy in the Church and the liturgy in life become one liturgy and true worship of God in Spirit and truth?

7. Read the mystical prayer offered by the priest before the Gospel, cited on p. 22 of the Study Guide, and answer these questions: What helps us to understand the message of the Gospel? What do we ask Christ to instill in our hearts as we listen to the Gospel? Why? How is a spiritual way of life defined by the prayer? What feelings and thoughts does this prayer inspire?

The Great Entrance

1. Explain the title, action, and purpose of the Great Entrance.

2. Discuss the symbolic and spiritual meaning of the Great Entrance on the basis of the Cherubic Hymn (p. 26 of the Study Guide). What Old Testament event does the Cherubic Hymn apply to the worshiping congregation? How can we truly receive Christ, the King of all?

3. What does it mean to acknowledge and confess Christ as King? How is this confession of faith reflected in our daily lives?

4. Why is it improper to kneel during the Great Entrance (despite its symbolic and spiritual significance)?

5. As the fruits of the earth, bread and wine, are brought to the Holy Altar Table during the Great Entrance, what personal gifts can you bring before the throne of God at that solemn moment?

6. What feelings and thoughts do you have when you hear the priest prayerfully chant during the Great Entrance: "May the Lord, our God, remember all of you (or us) in His kingdom, now and forever and to the ages of ages"?

The Offering of the Gifts (*Anaphora*)

1. The offering and consecration of the eucharistic gifts is preceded by the *Plerotika* (Completing Petitions), the Nicene Creed, and the kiss of peace. What is the meaning of each of these and how do they prepare the congregation for the offering of the gifts of bread and wine to God the Father? How does each of them apply to you?

2. What spiritual dispositions does the Liturgy require of us just before the great Eucharistic Prayer? How do they apply to you?

3. Name and give the significance of the six component parts of the Eucharistic Prayer.

4. What is the essence of the meaning of the offering and consecration of the eucharistic gifts? How does it apply to you?

5. What are your feelings and thoughts as you hear the priest chant, "Ta sa ek ton son" ("We offer to You these gifts from Your own gifts in all and for all") and you kneel in reverence?

6. What parts of the Eucharistic Prayer remind us that we are participants at the Last Supper and behold Christ Himself offering the gifts of bread and wine to God the Father?

7. Discuss the hymn "Se Imnoumen" ("We praise You, we bless You, we give thanks to You, and we pray to You, Lord our God"). Why do we praise, bless, and thank God at this moment? What is true praise and thanksgiving to God? What specifically are you thankful to God for? In what ways can all of life be a "eucharist" to God?

The Lord's Prayer

1. How often do you pray the Lord's Prayer? What feelings and thoughts does it inspire in you?

2. What kind of prayer is the Lord's Prayer (petition, intercession, penitential, thanksgiving, glorification, etc.)?

3. What does it mean to address God as "Father"? How does it apply to you?

4. Meditate on and discuss each part of the Lord's Prayer. How does each glorification and petition apply to you?

5. How do you define prayer? What is the purpose of prayer?

6. Why do many find it difficult to pray? What are these difficulties? How can they be overcome?

7. What benefits derive from prayer?

Holy Communion

1. How do you define the basic meaning of Holy Communion?

2. How often do you receive Holy Communion? Why or why not?

3. What feelings and thoughts do you have when you hear the priest's invitation and go forward to receive Holy Communion?

4. What impact or consequences does Holy Communion have in your life?

5. How can a person effectively prepare for Holy Communion?

6. Meditate on and discuss any of the Communion Prayers.

7. Read the following mystical prayer of thanksgiving offered by the priest after the congregation has received Holy Communion:

"We thank You, loving Master, benefactor of our souls, that on this day You have made us worthy once again of your heavenly and immortal Mysteries. Direct our ways in the right path, establish us firmly in Your fear, guard our lives, and make our endeavors safe, through the

prayers and supplications of the glorious Theotokos and ever virgin Mary and of all Your
saints."

Why are we thankful to Christ? What requests
do we make of Christ? What feelings and
thoughts does this prayer inspire?

The Dismissal

1. The dismissal is a final blessing of the congregation by the priest as the Liturgy concludes.
   What is the meaning of this blessing for our
   ordinary lives?

2. The priest prepares the congregation for dismissal by saying: "Let us go forth in peace!" How
   do we derive peace from the Liturgy? What does
   "go forth" imply for the faithful Christian?

3. In the Liturgy we often pray through the priest:
   "Let us commit ourselves, and one another, and
   our whole life to Christ our God." What does this
   statement mean to you? How does it apply
   specifically to your family, job, joys, and difficulties in life?

4. With what feelings and thoughts about yourself, your local Church, and life do you leave the
   Liturgy?

5. How can you help strengthen the bonds of love,
   unity, and common life of your local Church as
   a true family of God and the mystical body of
   Christ?

6. In what ways can you connect Liturgy to Liturgy
   and successfully resist the corroding influences
   of society during the week?

7. Study the following prayer offered by the priest
   at the dismissal:

   "Lord, bless those who praise You and
   sanctify those who put their trust in You. Save
   Your people and bless Your inheritance. Protect
   the whole body of Your Church. Sanctify those
   who love the beauty of Your house. Glorify them

in return by Your divine power, and do not forsake us who hope in You. Grant peace to Your world, to Your Churches, to the clergy, to those in public service, to the armed forces, and to all Your people. For every good and perfect gift is from above, coming from You, the Father of lights. To You we give glory, thanksgiving, and worship, to the Father and the Son and the Holy Spirit, now and forever and to the ages of ages."

How are the worshipers described in this prayer? What requests do we make of God? For whom, besides the congregation, do we pray? How is God described and why? What do we offer to God?

BIBLIOGRAPHY

FOR FURTHER STUDY:

Nicholas Cabasilas, *A Commentary on the Divine Liturgy.* London: SPCK, 1960.

Nicholas Cabasilas, *The Life in Christ.* Crestwood: St. Vladimir's Seminary Press, 1974.

Stanley S. Harakas, *Living the Liturgy.* Minneapolis: Light & Life, 1974.

Stanley S. Harakas, *The Melody of Prayer: How to Personally Experience the Divine Liturgy.* Minneapolis: Light and Life, 1979.

Augoustinos N. Kantiotes, *On the Divine Liturgy: Orthodox Homilies,* Vols. 1-2. ET, Asterios Gerostergios. Belmont: Institute for Byzantine and Modern Greek Studies, 1986.

Alexander Schmemann, *For the Life of the World: Sacraments and Orthodoxy.* Crestwood: St. Vladimir's Seminary Press, 1973.

Daniel J. Sheerin, *The Eucharist: Message of the Fathers of the Church.* Wilmington: Michael Glazier, 1986.